Overcoming Jealousy and Possessiveness

Overcoming Jealousy and Possessiveness

by
PAUL A. HAUCK

THE WESTMINSTER PRESS
Philadelphia

Book Design by Dorothy Alden Smith

First edition

Published by The Westminster Press ®
Philadelphia, Pennsylvania

PRINTED IN THE UNITED STATES OF AMERICA
9 8 7 6

Library of Congress Cataloging in Publication Data

Hauck, Paul A.
    Overcoming jealousy and possessiveness.

    1. Jealousy.   2. Possessiveness.   I. Title.
BF575.J4H38   179'.8   81-3040
ISBN 0-664-24374-6   AACR2

To Lena and Carmen

Contents

Preface

IN THE SPRING OF 1980 I RECEIVED A SUGGESTION FROM my publisher that I write a book on jealousy. It was proposed as an addition to my series of books on emotional problems starting with *Overcoming Depression.* The suggestion of the new title was "Overcoming Jealousy."

The more I thought about the proposal, the more intrigued I became. A book on jealousy and possessiveness had definite merit. A well thought out, coherent theory of jealousy according to rational emotive principles had yet to be offered. The challenge proved irresistible. So here I am again. I have been somewhat surprised at how frequently jealousy problems come up with clients in my daily practice. More than ever I am convinced that an uncomplicated book on the subject is needed to help the jealous person as well as those who are the victims of jealous persons.

Those of you who are acquainted with my other books will feel at home with this one. The full understanding of jealousy and possessiveness touches upon such disturbances as depression, anger, fear, and procrastination—all subjects I have covered fully before.

9

When further reading on such problems would be desirable, I will refer you to the books in question.

For whom am I writing this book? For all persons who suffer from these twin monsters—jealousy and possessiveness. So serious are these twisted emotions that children often drive themselves to distraction because of sibling rivalry; talented adults fail to progress up the vocational ladder because of the blatant mistakes they make with fellow workers or supervisors; lovely friendships are lost forever because one person fares better than another as the years roll by; and workable marriages are destroyed because fear and anger replace tenderness and understanding.

With the hope that some of these disasters can be averted through increased knowledge of the psychology of jealousy and possessiveness, I ask you to join me in the pages ahead. But first, lest we misunderstand each other, let me stress that not every expression of jealousy or possessiveness is worthy of concern. Few persons get all the attention and love they want from their mates. In the normal course of daily events these frustrations often lead to mild pangs of jealousy and reasonable efforts at greater possessiveness.

If you did not care in the slightest for someone, you could never be jealous no matter what attentions that person gave to someone else. It makes perfectly good sense, therefore, to become annoyed, saddened, or frustrated if your partner takes you to a dance and lets you sit by yourself most of the evening.

It also makes perfectly good sense to become annoyed, saddened, or frustrated if you want more time with your partner but somehow other matters keep interfering.

10

These normal emotional responses are healthy when they signal to you that your relationship is slightly off balance. Becoming aware of your annoyance, or sadness, or frustration urges you to do something about it. Usually you bring the matter up for discussion. Perhaps a compromise is reached that satisfies both parties. And from these efforts equilibrium is reestablished and harmony again prevails.

This book is not written for those whose jealousy or possessive problems are this manageable. They don't need the help. It is the intensely jealous and possessive person who can best use this book. It is those individuals who lose their self-control that I am addressing. Persons who become violent, who become physically sick with fear, who cannot conduct their daily affairs because of their obsessive thoughts—these are the people for whom I am writing this book. They are among the most wretched of all people; they are so blind about their behavior they cannot see themselves as their own destroyers. The persons referred to in this book are real, but their accounts to me have been altered to avoid loss of confidentiality without losing the essence of their experiences.

My special thanks go to Donna Ericson and Dorothy Meyer, who not only typed the manuscript but contributed to its readability.

P.A.H.

1
The Psychology of Jealousy and Possessiveness

HE WAS A YOUNG MAN IN HIS LATE TWENTIES, WITH A strong, handsome face. I tried to figure out what his problem was when he first came to my office, but for the life of me I had no idea. When he told me why he wanted help and how badly he needed it, I was taken by surprise.

He was one of the most jealous men I had ever met, and I've met quite a few. One client wouldn't let his wife visit a male physician. Another insisted that his wife call him many times a day so he could check up on her. But no one equaled Abner.

This man truly was desperate for his girl friend's love. If she didn't call him when she said she would, he left his office and drove over to her place to see whom she was sleeping with. He followed her around town, even when she was out with the girls. If she talked to a man at the bowling alley, he'd get the man's name somehow and confront her with it later.

She couldn't converse with or smile at another man. She even had to be careful she didn't give too much attention to her children from a former marriage, lest he give her the third degree. And his third degrees were really something. They'd last late into the night, until Ruby, in tears, was willing to admit to anything just to bring the matter to a close. But once she did that, Abner was off on another tack, asking her for more and more details of what she did, with whom, and when she was "going to be open and honest" with him.

What happened to Abner and Ruby? They broke up. He was furious with me because I didn't get his Ruby to love him more. He went to another therapist, who had no more success than I did. So what happened?

Abner wound up in jail after beating up a man Ruby went out with one night. The policeman who tried to arrest him got assaulted for his effort. Eventually Abner lost his job, lost his girl, and lost his freedom. He's in the state penitentiary with a broken heart.

Now let's study another case, this time of possessiveness. Sylvia did not worry about Ralph's going with other women. He was a loyal husband. Her problem was that she wanted to control his life so completely that she'd have his constant companionship. I couldn't quite understand why she needed him around almost all the time since she was a good-looking woman with loads of friends.

Somewhere, deep in her mind, she felt threatened if she was not in control of Ralph and if he found more pleasure with others.

Over the years of their marriage she managed to keep Ralph dependent on her. Seldom did she encourage him to cook a meal for himself, do a load of laundry, iron a shirt, or write out a check. She loved to mother him, and Ralph, unaware that he was being lured into a baby crib, went right along with her, feeling privileged and pampered most of the time.

As he got older, however, Ralph wanted more freedom. He made moves to do things without getting Sylvia's approval or without even telling her about his plans. This put the fear of God into Sylvia and she responded by getting him back in line and tightening up the controls.

"Whither thou goest, I will go," comes from The Book of Ruth. That could have been Sylvia's motto. She didn't let Ralph breathe until he asked her if he could. She selected his clothes; she even drew his bath.

This marriage survived, last I heard. Ralph learned to toe the line and do as he was told. That pleased Sylvia so much she quieted down. They were grateful to me for keeping their marriage together. Down deep I felt our therapy would have been more successful if they had separated.

A jealous person gives the impression of being a very self-confident person. After all, these individuals act like generals about to charge the enemy. There is absolutely nothing squeamish about them. They seem to know exactly what they want and they fight like savages to get it. They order their partners around as though the latter were children. They argue late into the night for their point of view. Nothing anyone can say to them seems to have the slightest effect on their reasoning. If the phone rings but no one is on the line, they know something furtive is going on behind the scene. "That's why you were late from work by about fifteen minutes." These are not accidents. They are proof. The jealous and possessive person is totally convinced.

Can you guess what personality characteristic lies behind such behavior? It is an inferiority complex of mammoth dimensions. Although the symptoms may be hid-

15

den, feelings of inferiority are among the major characteristic traits of jealous and possessive people. I have loosely identified six strong characteristics of jealous and possessive people, but this feature is the driving force behind all the others.

Inferiority Complex

If you get jealous, even just a bit, it is because you think too little of yourself. You have learned a bad psychological act, and you have learned to do it very well. Which act? Self-blame.

You judge yourself by your actions, your performance, your achievements, your friends, and your possessions. You literally believe you are better as a human being because you are better-looking, or smarter, or richer, or more talented. To you, a person and the person's behavior are inseparable. If you get a promotion (which is clear proof of your vocational talent), you suddenly and miraculously also think you are a better person. And if you lose a job, or your money, or your good looks, you conclude you're less of a person.

You'd have to do that, wouldn't you? If we as persons are inseparable from everything connected with us, then it makes sense to damn or praise ourselves depending upon what happens to us.

Blame, as I use the term psychologically, means that you have attacked yourself in two ways: *(a)* for not having success, or money, or love, and *(b)* then concluding that you, *as a total human being,* are worthless and inferior. That's how the inferiority complex originates and maintains itself.

One of the most unfortunate standards you, the jeal-

16

ous person, use to judge worthiness is whether or not you are loved. Approval or disapproval by a loved one means the same to you as the Roman emperor's thumb meant to the gladiator in the Colosseum: thumb up and his life was saved, thumb down and he was instantly killed.

Rejection is the big monster, the boogeyman, the adult spook by which you scare yourself. And, like those innocent childhood fears, rejection too is perfectly harmless. Being unloved as an adult is only uncomfortable, inconvenient, and sad. It is not something to get panicky over, to get violent about, or a cause to drink yourself into oblivion.

Spend your energies on changing your self-downing techniques and you'll be doing something far more sane for yourself than your jealousy accomplishes. Accept yourself truly and it won't matter all that much who else accepts you.

The Master-Slave Mentality

Just as inferiority is the foundation of jealousy, the cornerstone of the jealous personality has to be the master-slave mentality. It is the rare jealous or possessive person who suffers emotional pangs in silence. Most jealous persons register their grievances loudly and clearly. They scream at their partners, smack them around, and hassle them shamelessly. Couples get into shouting matches when the husband or wife feels neglected. Men have smashed their own furniture or put their fists through walls, and women have smashed dishes and thrown food, all in an effort to make their complaints appreciated.

17

These can be momentary eruptions of emotions which quiet down in a matter of minutes or hours, followed by calm deliberations between the two warring parties. The deeply jealous and possessive person is not nearly so easy to live with. That person has a dangerous and undemocratic philosophy which he or she thinks is completely justified. In short, the philosophy is dictatorship and slavery, with the jealous person as dictator and slave driver.

You doubt this? You think I exaggerate to make a point? Then listen to some of the comments a woman once made to me.

THERAPIST: Mabel, what is it like to live with a jealous person?

CLIENT: I have to struggle against his feelings of inadequacy all the time. If I go to church with the kids, he really gets mad because I won't stay home with him. He wants my total attention.

T: What did you do?

C: I tried staying home all the time, but he doesn't apply the same rules for me that apply to him. He can go out if he wants, but I had better be home when he gets back.

T: Where does he go?

C: He goes wherever he wants—to bars, on trips. He's even gone for a week or more.

T: Without you or the kids?

C: Yes. He'd apologize at first, and I always forgave him, hoping he would grow out of it in time. But he never did. It's getting worse.

T: How do you mean?

C: I can't talk to my girl friends, even over the phone.

18

He pulls the receiver right out of my hands. He always wants to know what I'm talking about on the phone, or what was said in letters to me by my brother. He always felt I was talking about him. I'd wind up losing, no matter what I did.

T: How so?

C: If I agreed with his accusations, he'd get angry and maybe beat me. If I denied his accusations, he'd get angry and beat me. You can't win.

Do you see the point? Jealous persons literally feel that their partners are merchandise, property with which they can do anything they want. They think they own people, the way they own their cars.

They care not one bit about the feelings of others, only their own. There are two sets of rules in their philosophy: rules for themselves, and a second set for others. And you don't have to be a genius to figure out who gives the orders and who is expected to obey.

A slave owner thinks that slaves have no rights but that the slave owner has a God-given right to demand anything from the slave, and that these rights ought to be enforced with violence if need be.

Can you imagine such unfairness? After slavery was outlawed by all civilized governments one hundred years ago, it's ironic that it often crops up right within the family circle.

Self-Defeating Behavior

One of the most amazing characteristics of jealous and possessive persons is that they are psychologically blind. Yet these people are often bright, sophisticated, schooled, and beautiful. They are capable and outstanding in many areas of their lives. But when it comes to their loved ones, the jealous individuals actually act as though they were retarded.

For example, suppose you couldn't pay your rent and were about to be evicted, baggage and all, and you then found a paper bag full of money. What would you do with some of it? If you're a reasonably bright person, and not hell-bent on hurting yourself, you'd quickly give your landlord what you owe and then put the rest in the bank. But what if you took that windfall and threw a wild party, or bet it on the horses, or went on a vacation and did not pay your rent? Would you call that smart behavior? If you would, friend, you have a problem.

Self-defeating behavior is characteristic of the jealous and possessive person. You have no enemy worse than yourself and here is why I say this: Without fail you drive away, with enormous energy, the very people whose love you fear losing. You don't do just a few things to annoy your lover. You become a positive pain, a whining, crying, screaming child who honestly believes that you must have what you want at any cost. Though you know better, you will act in exact opposition to the way required to get someone to love you.

I don't for a moment want to sound blaming or rejecting when I use such strong terms. I have the utmost respect for all people regardless of their emotional makeup. No one is perfect and therefore I don't expect perfect behavior. But that does not alter the fact that jealous people do act unwisely when it comes to solving their love problems.

Take Jim as an example. His wife went back to work

a year before I saw the couple. Their children were in school all day, so she wanted to get out of the house and meet people. Those in her office were a congenial bunch. They all lunched together, stopped off together for a few drinks after work on Fridays, and had parties during the holidays.

This blew Jim's mind. He became so threatened by her exposure to other people (women included) that he insisted she quit her job. He'd badger her, accuse her of falling in love with every man in the office, trying to make her feel as guilty as possible. He even threatened to have an affair, to get drunk, to leave her, to kill himself, or to divorce her. Since she felt she was totally innocent, she couldn't give in to any of these demands.

In counseling, I tried to get him to see that if he kept up his attack, his suspicions of her might indeed come true. "The more you accuse her, the less she'll love you," I warned. "Keep quiet about your suspicions. You've made your feelings known. Now say nothing. If she continues to work and you eventually find out she's unfaithful, then, and only then, divorce her if you want to. Until then trust her completely."

He wouldn't listen. Not once did he let up. I could see the marriage disintegrating right before my eyes. It didn't take long before she became indifferent to his complaints. Her love for him was rapidly slipping away. Instead of backing off as any sensible person would, he got twice as nasty.

"You're going to lose her if you don't stop," I again warned him. "The harder you push, the less she loves you."

"But I must have her love. I can't stand the thought of losing her. She's my whole life."

"Then be nice and loving. If you don't, you'll push her into the arms of another man, not because she necessarily wants that, but because you've become so unlovable."

Isn't this simplicity itself? To expect love from someone when you are hateful, mean, nasty, or violent is just silly. But that's what Jim did. All by himself he achieved the very thing he most dreaded: the loss of his wife's love.

If that isn't being blind and self-defeating, what is? Listen to what he said to his wife one day:

"I was scared to death you wouldn't come home. When you did I was furious with myself for not trusting you. How dumb can one get? You're the one person I want to be close to. I want to be the person you come to when you need help. I love you desperately and get frightened at the very thought of losing you. You're the finest person who ever entered my life. I'm nothing without you. Help me! Forgive me!"

Difficulty in Accepting Responsibility

One of the most startling personality traits found among jealous and possessive persons is their great difficulty in accepting responsibility for their jealousy. Almost without fail they accuse their mates of making them miserable by tormenting them, by dancing with others, talking to others, complimenting others, or even looking at others. Rarely do they glimpse the reality of their problem: that *they* themselves are largely responsible for their problems and *totally responsible* for their own feelings of jealousy.

If you are the jealous partner, does the following description apply to you? First, you absolutely believe that your emotional disturbance is caused by your partner. Even though people have been telling you differently for some time, you still insist that your mate is the reason for your jealousy. His conversations with others drive you insane. Her phone calls with the chairman of the picnic committee make you see green. And so on.

You are wrong. Even if she makes love with her old flame right in front of you, that won't make you jealous unless you let it. Granted, it is not proper behavior for a wife. And for you to disapprove of it and to be saddened by it would be perfectly normal. However, to become filled with rage and want to kill someone is neurotic. And you are the only one who can do that to yourself.

The sane thing to do when you believe your partner does not love you is to find out what he or she wants from you. Then if you can satisfy those deep desires and needs, do so and watch the changes in attitude toward you. If your partner doesn't change, you have rather good evidence that he or she has fallen out of love for good. In either case those actions are both better than turning green with jealousy.

Most jealous persons don't have that much self-control. If you are the jealous one, you stubbornly insist that *(a)* your mate must admit he or she is upsetting you, *(b)* he or she must do something about *your* jealousy, and *(c)* then you will have peace of mind again.

This analysis has things backward. First, no one can make you jealous: it comes from the *way you think about your lover's behavior,* not the behavior itself.

Secondly, why don't you do something about your own jealousy instead of shoving that responsibility off

23

on your lover? If that emotion is giving you such a bad time, I would think you'd want to change it in every way you could. On the contrary, you insist on only one way: your mate must stay home, must not smile at others, must never be late, must always do what you require. That places the responsibility for your relief, not upon you *who have the problem,* but upon your partner *who doesn't have the problem.* Why don't you see a counselor to help you deal with your own jealousy?

Stop expecting your lover to do something you won't even do. If you don't care enough to address your own problem, then why should anyone else care?

The eternal theme song of the jealous and possessive person is that the mate, partner, or lover cannot be trusted. That's why who is talking with whom is always such an issue. It is a matter of distrust: a deep conviction that anyone wearing pants is going to steal the wife away, and that anyone in a skirt can steal the husband away.

Seldom does it dawn on you, the insecure person, that the distrust is actually of two kinds: distrust of your lover *and* distrust of yourself. It is the distrust you feel about yourself, however, that causes the jealousy, not the distrust of the lover.

Though you may be correct about some of the people who are trying to ruin your love life, this is largely a figment of your imagination. How many of us have husbands or wives that the whole population is panting to seduce? You flatter yourself to suppose that everyone has the same taste in beauty you have. Relax. Your mate may be the apple of *your* eye but in all likelihood would only be applesauce for others.

There is another reason why distrust of your lover is

24

seldom justified. My own observations as a clinical psychologist of twenty-seven years' experience convinces me that faithfulness between two committed persons is still the norm. The sexual revolution has not changed the deep desire of most people to have an enduring relationship with one person at a time. What has changed since the sexual revolution is the ease with which people will seek out other partners when it becomes evident that their current love relationships are going sour. Then, and often not until then, will men and women seek other lovers. This tendency is most pronounced for the partners of jealous and possessive persons. And small wonder.

Incidentally, people usually don't deceive their lovers with delight and joy. Whether it be a one-night stand, an affair, or a divorce, these involvements occur after many sleepless nights, much regret and even anguish, and finally a feeling of resignation. By the time a new romance is even seriously contemplated, a million dreams have been trampled under the heels of a thoughtless lover or a lover who, despite valiant effort, was not able to please the partner sufficiently.

If you cannot apply this analysis to your love relationship, perhaps your partner is one of those persons who require a change in lovers every so often. Variety is the spice of their sex life. In that case, you have cause to be distrustful. However, that is about the only instance in which you have a rational right to be distrustful.

Otherwise your distrust arises from deep within your solid conviction that you are unlovable, that your partner must see you as undesirable because you feel that nearly everyone else is more desirable. That's your problem. If you don't regard yourself as worthwhile, it

25

is easily understandable why you would be convinced that others couldn't regard you in a kindly light either.

Your task, therefore, is to overcome your jealousy, not by trying to force others to love you more, but by hating yourself less. That's hard to do, I grant. Nevertheless it is possible. More importantly, it is the most reasonable option you have, because it will work wonders if you do it.

Your present methods of checking up on your lover, throwing accusations left and right, breaking dishes and furniture have not worked, are not working now, and will never work in the future.

Selfishness and Immaturity

A fifth common personality trait found among severely jealous persons is selfishness. Under this heading comes a whole host of other features that go hand in hand with selfishness. Before I describe them, let me make an important distinction between being selfish and being self-interested.

The selfish person wants his or her way without considering the desires or needs of the other person. These transactions are all one-way streets. "Give me, give me, give me. Nuts to you. Whatever I want I have to have." The notion of reciprocity is foreign to these persons.

Theirs is the mentality of the child who has not learned to share, to repay a service, to put the desires of others first for a reasonable amount of the time. It is a neurotic emotion.

Being self-interested, however, is healthy. It places you and your desires above those of others at times. But it never does so without your realizing that a favor will someday have to be repaid. The self-interested person knows there is no free lunch. If you are invited to your friend's house for dinner, your sense of social etiquette compels you to invite your friend back for a dinner, not just for a can of beer or a cup of coffee.

The self-interested person can appear to others to be selfish when a decided-upon course of action may seriously displease the partner. The wife may insist she will get a job despite her husband's protests, but she knows she will have to remain silent when he wants to do his thing.

There you have the test you can apply to any dispute in which you are accused of being selfish. Are you willing to *(a)* return the favor, *(b)* or allow a privilege similar to the one you are asking for? If you are, you need not feel the slightest bit of guilt, because you can always claim you are being completely fair and just. If you can't say that much, you probably are being selfish.

Now, what about you when you are the jealous and possessive person? Your problem is that you are practically always selfish when something goes wrong in your love life. During millions of other moments you can be considerate, generous, and wonderfully mature. You have as much tenderness as the next person when your lover is injured, when your child cries, or when your neighbor wants to borrow your mower.

However, when your lover shows any interest (not love, just interest) in anyone or anything that does not make you the center of attention even for a brief while, then the green-eyed monster rears its ugly head. That's when you don't care about anyone's welfare but your own.

One man I counseled was just about the most one-sided, selfish mate a woman could possibly have.

He wanted her to walk with her eyes to the ground like a nun, not talk to fellow workers, not be friendly with anyone, not answer the phone politely. He wanted her to talk only to women and to eat lunch alone. He even forbade her to accept kisses and hugs from her mother or father. He demanded that she break off with old friends, look straight ahead when driving a car, and acquiesce to a host of other impossible and ridiculous requests.

When his wife suggested he was unreasonable, he reacted as though she were speaking Swahili. He had no concept of how selfish, demanding, and immature he was.

If you're going to be jealous, try to be civil in the process. Suffer silently with your neurosis rather than thrust it upon those whom you believe are rejecting you. Then, while you are nursing your deep pains, learn how to overcome your hurts, be they depressive feelings of self-blame or self-pity, or angry feelings of revenge, or fearful feelings such as worry, tension, or nervousness. Learn also how to be a more loving person, so that your partner will find you more compatible. Learn how to accept yourself whether or not your partner (or anyone else, for that matter) loves you in return. Then your miseries will at least be confined just to you (a real blessing), and you will be on a self-improvement program that cannot hurt you a bit and can help you enormously.

But, alas, most people who suffer jealousy and possessiveness are anything but private about it. If they get an attack in a public bar, they haven't the slightest qualm about staging a nasty scene. It doesn't matter who is

28

present—family, friends, or strangers. These folks crusade toward the ruination of their loving relationships like lemmings heading for suicide in the sea.

Why do they do this? Why do they upset their children, terrorize their mates in the wee hours of the mornings, and cry on the shoulders of almost anyone who will listen to their woes?

Because they are angry and believe that their lovers are bad people who must be punished. They sincerely believe they themselves should never be frustrated, rejected, or threatened in any way. They honestly feel that others do not have the right to change their minds, that once they profess love for someone, they must keep their pledges no matter what may happen.

Who said so? Why must people do as they promise? Why can't people go back on their word? Because it's immoral and unethical? Is that why? Nonsense! It is right and proper to keep a promise if you make one. It is also regrettably inevitable for a human being at times to be unethical and immoral. In other words, *everyone has the right to be wrong,* whether we like it or not. Incidentally, that comes in rather handy when you and I are also badly mistaken or acting stupidly.

You see, anger is the result of your making *neurotic demands* out of healthy wishes. It is precisely parallel to what a child does when the child does not get what is wished for. The youngster wants a lollipop and mother says "No." The child instantly changes the wish into a demand and has a temper tantrum. Why? Because the youngster did not get what was *wanted?* No. Because the child didn't get what was *demanded.*

You do the same thing every time you get angry. Anger is an adult temper tantrum. However, you do not get upset over not getting lollipops or ice-cream cones. You get upset over not getting all the love and attention you erroneously think you need. *Your* lollipop is having your mate by your side all evening at a party instead of your mate talking to old buddies or a few women friends. *Wanting* your mate not to do this is one thing. *Insisting* on it is quite another.

As a jealous person you often make perfectly normal, reasonable, and sane requests. When you get mad and bitter because you aren't getting your way, *no matter what the issue,* you are then acting like a child who also thinks it's not just inconvenient or annoying but intolerable if you don't get what you want.

In the following conversation a young mother tells me how her husband reacted when she told him she was unhappy. Notice especially how absolutely blind he is about his own behavior. Not for a moment does it dawn on him that everything he did after she told him she loved him less positively had to make her dislike him more.

CLIENT: He kept asking me what I was so unhappy about. Finally I told him I just didn't know if I cared that much for him anymore. A lot of things had happened in the seven years of our marriage, and I had just gotten to the point where I didn't know whether it was worth it or not to continue the relationship.

He got badly upset. He threw a fit at me and the kids. Then he tried to calm down, and we went for a walk and we tried to talk. But when it came time to go to bed, he just got upset again.

I was afraid of him. I was afraid of what he might do to me. He ended up pushing me out of the house.

30

He kept telling me to get my stuff together and if I didn't, he would.

I called my parents and I said I was going to stay all night. When I got up the next morning, I found the porch piled high with my clothes, just thrown there. There was no way I could sort out anything so that I could get dressed to go to the shop.

First, I called the foreman and told him I wouldn't be in because I didn't feel well. Then I drove home and my husband was outside and he wouldn't let me in. He said I should just go on back to my mom's house and stay there. I said, "No. I want to see the kids." He went back in the house, and I followed him. Then he called up his office and said he was having some problems and would come in later. He called my folks again and said, "Can she bring all her stuff over to your house and put it somewhere?" I told him I wasn't going to leave, that it was my house too.

THERAPIST: What did he say?

C: He told me I had to, that unless I called a lawyer, I would have to leave. I told him I didn't have to leave and wasn't going to. He said that he was going to change the locks. If I could never get back in, and if he was mad enough, I figured he could just say I deserted him and the kids. I wouldn't have my kids or anything. So I said, "No, I am not going to leave." And all the time he was asking: "Why don't you love me anymore? If you don't, you are just going to have to leave. You can't stay here." He kept saying: "Why? There has got to be a reason why. Why, all of a sudden, don't you care about me?" And then I told him about all the ways he hurt me and cared more about himself than about me and the children. He got mad,

31

madder than before. So I pointed that out to him again. "See? That's what I mean. I'm afraid of you. I don't love you. How could I?"

Then he smacked me and I fell. That's when I decided to leave him.

T: Could he see how he brought that on himself?
C: Now, yes. Then, no.

Fearfulness

Another characteristic typical of jealous people is their tendency to feel threatened by the most innocent of events. Almost anything can set off these otherwise fine and decent people.

There is no conceivable way that their families, friends, or lovers can behave so perfectly that the jealous persons won't feel threatened by some totally innocent act.

Study these two examples. First, a woman buys a new dress. Her husband has never seen it. In the evening as they are getting ready to go out, the doorbell rings. He is putting on his tie, so she answers the door. It is the couple they are going out with that evening. The man makes a flattering comment to her about her appearance the moment he enters the house with his wife. It's all polite and innocent.

But to her husband it wasn't. He misjudged the scene completely, felt needlessly afraid his buddy was making a pass at his wife and could not be persuaded otherwise even after hours of quarreling later that evening.

The second example is of a woman who felt quite comfortable with her husband's career as long as he socialized with persons who were no better educated or no more sophisticated than she was. She was always a supportive wife. She helped her husband through college, entertained as she needed to advance his career, and seemed to be a stable person who knew precisely what she was doing. Her marriage seemed idyllic, especially when she was told one day that he had been given a major promotion.

Ironically that proved to be the beginning of her problem. Her husband now dressed better, ate lunch in the executive dining room, and mingled with people of success, sophistication, and travel. She now perceived him as growing beyond her. While he was becoming Mr. Big Shot, she remained "just his wife, whom he doesn't need anymore."

Nothing he could do could give her peace of mind. Because she defined worthiness for herself as being someone who must be needed by her husband, she felt frightened, and threatened by his success.

Isn't that a shame? They both worked hard for years to get to where they fulfilled their dreams and then her exquisite sensitivity turned it into a nightmare.

Jealous people are practically paranoid considering all the little things at which they take offense. Who else would go to pieces because a partner loses weight? That's normal for fearful men and women. The more attractive the lover becomes, the more uneasy the partner becomes. There is a growing feeling of inability to compete against all the people who are going to flirt or seduce the mate.

I've counseled many couples who had serious troubles because one mate was trying to socialize with a different class of people. Accusations made by the jealous person went as follows: "Who do you think you are?

Mrs. Vanderbilt?" "What makes you think those people want to mix with the likes of you or me?" "Aren't you forgetting yourself? Why don't you keep your place?"

All these utterances are intended for one thing only: to discourage competition. That's how fearful jealous people are. For them, competition and the possible loss of the loved one are constant obsessions. They are like individuals who have committed crimes and who suspect the police are watching them from every corner. Or they are like persons who were frightened as children and have never gotten over their fear of ghosts, of dogs, or of being alone.

The fear of being rejected, unloved, and therefore of becoming nothing is so strong that these persons suffer all their lives.

To give a better picture of how frightened people can be about not being loved, this verbal transcript is cited with permission.

"I really don't know where to begin except by saying 'Help.' I am at the end of my rope and I'm slipping. My soul seems to be branded with a fear, a fear so deeply rooted that it is agonizing. It tears at me and tortures me so that I know it will someday kill me.

"When my boyfriend looks at another woman I go into a frenzy, a frenzy so uncontrollable that it cuts him like a knife and it tears at me as if it were the devil himself.

"When all the beautiful women with their voluptuous breasts lie naked in front of his eyes on the television screen I die a thousand deaths. Or when he looks through a girlie magazine I almost go off the deep end. To think that he stared at those women made me feel so ugly outside and inside.

"I have asked God to help me, but the Lord only helps those who help themselves, and I can't help myself. I can't enjoy life anymore. I used to smile at every person I met. Now I feel like I'm dying.

"Please, please, please, I implore you for any help you can give."

None of this is necessary. Jealousy is always the same no matter where you find it: *(a)* a neurotic need for approval, and *(b)* an intense feeling of inferiority. If you conquer those two conditions, nothing, not even having someone sleep with your partner, can make you jealous. In fact, you could have several people sleep with your partner on a regular basis and still not feel jealous if you did not have problems with inferiority feelings and a neurotic need for approval.

Must There Be Jealousy?

It is assumed that jealousy has to be a natural behavior of humans, because it is so widespread. No matter where you go in the world you encounter it. The sophisticated European is often just as jealous as the backwoods trapper. The college professor can be as threatened by a compliment to his wife as is the stevedore. Beautiful people can be as upset over attentions paid to their partners as ugly people are.

Jealousy occurs not only between an adult man and woman. It also occurs with great frequency among brothers, among sisters, or between brothers and sisters. The Cain and Abel story is the most famous example of sibling jealousy. The jealousy that older children in the family have for the youngest, who is often the most spoiled, is also frequent.

35

Jealousy between parent and child is less common, but not so rare that I don't encounter it also from time to time. In one instance the parent is jealous of the child's youth and beauty. In another, the child is jealous of the parent's power and sophistication. A letter from a former female client contains the following:

"I will try to give you my observations of my daughter as best I can. Up to about the age of ten she was the sweetest child in the world. As soon as she entered puberty something happened to her. She changed so completely that I could not recognize her. I suppose all children change, but with her it was somehow different. I saw hate in her eyes. She turned against me in frequent rages. She would not let me kiss or hug her. Showering her with gifts did nothing for this problem.

"At fifteen, she frequently compared herself to me and felt she was skinny and ugly and would never develop like me. As she grew she developed into a beauty, but she kept finding fault with her eyebrows, or teeth, or other things.

"When I received a compliment from my family or her friends, she would be furious with me. I learned to avoid compliments so she wouldn't be threatened, but even this didn't help. Now that she is married we are farther apart than ever. I repeatedly asked for explanations but got none. She could hurt me by cutting me out of her life and this she did. She even gloated over it. Apparently it made her feel superior to me—finally."

A small group of young adults in San Francisco call themselves The Kerista Village. Currently the group consists of five women and three men. They sleep freely and willingly with each other on a regular schedule. No one is jealous. This is quite evident, because the group has been alive and well for nine years.

Outsiders are asked to join the group with the consent of all the members. The members must feel positive about a new applicant or he or she is rejected.

If nine persons can do this, why not 90 million (not live in such a commune, but live without jealousy)?

The Mormons did it for years. Brigham Young had many wives. Some of the wives may have been jealous, but surely not all of them were.

And what about the many wives of bygone African chieftains? If they could reach that level of sophistication, why can't we? (Again, I'm not referring to polygamy, only to the ability to conquer jealousy.)

Clarifying the Terms

The four terms "jealousy," "possessiveness," "envy," and "suspicion" are only vaguely understood by the average reader. That is of little consequence, in most instances, until you personally suffer from the first two or are the victim of the first two. In that event you had better get a clear idea of these emotional conditions and precisely how they differ. But let's take them in slightly different order.

Envy. This can be a healthy emotion because it can spur you on to achieve goals you might easily ignore.

In the spring of 1980 I happened to have lunch with two psychiatrists, both of whom were addicted to running. During our lunch I learned that they regularly ran a mile in seven minutes and fifteen or twenty seconds, whereas I normally ran a mile in ten, nine, or even eight minutes. These men were younger than I, but not by much. I instantly became envious of their stamina, speed, and physical fitness. I determined to run two seven-minute miles if I possibly could. So far I have managed twice to run a mile in seven and one half minutes, and I'm still going strong. The feeling is great and I'm proud of my achievement. I'm not jealous of their times, I only wish I could do as well. That's envy.

Jealousy. If I had resented their running skills and wanted to be the only one to run well, that would have been jealousy. The jealous person always wants to deny the other person whatever it is that is desired. One's sense of security rests on being the sole owner of something, or the best at something, or the only person in a particular position or relationship. The person is extremely uncomfortable until that comes about.

If you resent your wife's dancing with another man, you are indicating feelings of jealousy. You think she should enjoy dancing *only* with you. She should never laugh at another man's jokes, or enjoy any company but your own. You are jealous. If you were envious, you'd be saying to yourself: "Wow, that fellow looks great out there on the dance floor. He and my wife look like a great couple. I wish I could dance as well as he does."

But no, you distrust yourself. You feel so unsure of yourself that you are convinced every man can beat your time. Then you become a dictator and forbid your wife to do certain things so that you can claim her undivided attention and be reassured that you are the one and only in her life. Jealousy is always a neurotic emotion.

Possessiveness. This emotion is similar to jealousy, but in this case no third party is involved. You demand constant attention and companionship from your partner, not because you fear losing him or her to someone else, but because you think of yourself as less of a person without the love of your mate.

Possessive persons do not know what to do with themselves. Left alone, they feel abandoned, like children whose parents have deserted them. It can be painful, to be sure, but it arises from the same source that jealousy springs from, namely, the excessive need for love. Possessive persons believe they are worthwhile only when someone loves them and proves it by devoting all attentions to them.

Jealousy and possessiveness are extremely self-defeating emotions. Unlike envy, which helps you achieve your goals, jealousy and possessiveness help you lose your goals. The more compulsive you become about having love, the less likely you are to get it. The smothering, the anger, the dictatorial control, and above all, the blatant inferiority which underlies these feelings make you anything but Mate of the Year.

These are the words of a typically possessive woman: "I want him with me all the time. I'm mad when he isn't home. I want him doing something with me. When he would be gone, I would tense up and get nervous and angry and I know this builds up in me and we would have an argument every two weeks. I had this when I was married before. Every two weeks I have to blow up. I don't know why. Maybe not enough attention; I have to know that he loves me. If he yells at me, I know he loves me. I am testing him. If he leaves—that would prove he didn't love me. But if he stays and argues and accepts my finding fault with him or accepts my criticizing him, that is proof that he does."

Suspicion. If you think your lover is falling for your best friend, that's not necessarily a sign that you are

39

jealous. It may well be happening.

Is he spending more time away from home? Does he seem to have less money? Has his sex drive slowed down over the last few months? Are you getting phone calls and there is no one on the line? All these could be legitimate signs that something is seriously wrong between you two. There need not be jealous utterances at all.

If not converted into jealous feelings, suspicions can be thought of as acute observations, intelligent guess-work, and smart detective snooping. As such, they are healthy feelings warning you of danger. Don't dismiss them. But don't convert them to jealousy either.

A Case in Point: Ted and Amy

The following dialogue clearly presents many of the characteristics of jealous persons.

CLIENT: Last night Amy and I were going for a casual walk, when I met a former girl friend. I said, "Hi," and talked to her a moment. Amy said, "Who is that?" and I told her it was an old friend. Amy said, "Why did you talk to her?" I said I was just being friendly. She said, "All right, then I will do the same thing." I said, "Do whatever you want to, it won't bother me." She said, "Our engagement is off." I said: "You have got to be joking. We are so close to getting married. I can't believe it."

I felt bad about it the next day. Throwing all that away—an upcoming marriage—all because of her jealousy. It is hard for me to comprehend that. Right now I am a little leery of getting married at all.

THERAPIST: Do you think she is going to change after you marry her?

C: I don't know.

T: Is that what you are willing to live with?

C: I don't think so.

T: But that's what you may get.

C: Last Sunday we had gone for a few drinks with her girl friend. Amy was jealous because Sue and I both work in sales, and we have something in common. Now Amy says, "Why don't you take her out?" I don't have any desire to take Sue out. I've got to really watch what I say around Amy so I don't upset her.

T: Some problems are so unpleasant that it doesn't make any sense to marry someone with them.

C: Do you think she would ever be happy with anybody? Or would she be that way with everybody?

T: Let me just say that generally anybody who is a jealous person is jealous because of a lack of self-trust. Such persons think everybody is out to beat them. They think they are inferior to everybody and therefore they read threats into every smile, into every wave, into every remark.

C: I know she does feel inferior, because she has mentioned that she is "nothing but a mere factory worker." I think that is partly why she doesn't feel important.

T: That's right. She just doesn't think a great deal of herself. That's why she is convinced that you can't really like her. She can't believe it.

C: You don't think that getting married to me would give her more confidence?

T: Not a bit. What's that got to do with it?

C: Security.

41

T: You have given her assurance that you care for her, and that you love her, and so on. Has that convinced her she is truly lovable?

C: She doesn't think so.

T: That's my point. She can't believe that she's a lovable person. She's a bright, gorgeous, fine human being, but the problem is—who doesn't believe that?

C: She doesn't.

T: She doesn't, that's right. Until you can get her to believe it, nobody is going to convince her.

Notice how typical Amy is of all seriously jealous people. She is sensitive. Ted can't say hello to an old friend without Amy's feeling threatened. She is angry and impulsive, a veritable dictator: "Don't be nice to old friends or I won't marry you." That's probably the last thing she wants, but she'll practically push him away regardless. She feels inferior: any contact he has with another woman, even if it is of the most innocent kind, is enough to send her into orbit.

She defeats herself all by herself. She brings about the loss of his love as surely as the sun will rise tomorrow.

Notice also how she expects him to make all the changes so that she can gain relief. Not once does it occur to her that she has a problem for which she could get help. Instead, she places all the responsibility for *her* well-being on *him*.

Needless to say, this relationship has only a slim chance of surviving.

2
Ways to Correct Jealousy by Yourself

PEOPLE ARE OFTEN RELUCTANT TO GO INTO COUNSEL-
ing because they fear what might be discovered. Not
only that. They also frighten themselves with the
thought that if something "horrible" were discovered
during counseling, they wouldn't be able to do anything
about it. Small wonder people avoid self-knowledge.

Fortunately there is little truth in these beliefs. First
of all, the sort of things you will learn about yourself in
counseling are not all *that* unusual. You'll discover that
you are sensitive, or afraid of rejection, or a perfection-
ist, and so on. So what? There has to be something
wrong with you or you'd be floating in orbit around the
earth with a pair of wings.

Secondly, who says you can't do anything about your
shortcomings? Why do you have to be saddled with an
emotional problem forever because you've had it for
many years?

It's not true that behavior is unchangeable. Very few
habits cannot be modified. Stop and think of individuals
you know who have smoked several packs of cigarettes
a day and when they were told by their physician they
had to stop, they did so overnight. The same has hap-

pened to persons who had a long history of drinking or involvement with drugs. Don't minimize those accomplishments. Such habits are difficult to break.

So why can't personality habits be changed? That's actually what a counselor does—teaches clients to change personality habits. Anger, depression, worry, procrastination, and jealousy can all be overcome.

Remember this statement: *What you learn you can unlearn.* The fact that you could learn to behave in an unpleasant way means only that you were a good student but had a poor teacher. You picked up those teachings as a youngster when your ability to question the teacher was weak. That is no longer the case. Today you are an adult. You can think for yourself. You don't have to believe everything you were taught when you were young.

Use your intelligence and question the notion *(a)* that you must be perfect to be worthwhile; *(b)* that you must be loved to be worthwhile; and *(c)* that others' behavior can directly upset you.

The moment you stop believing these irrational ideas is the moment your habit changes for the better.

You learned to be a jealous and possessive person. You weren't born that way. And you aren't "naturally" that way. Never say: "That's my nature. I can't help it. I've always been jealous."

Say instead: "I learned to rate myself and to compare myself with my behavior. I learned to think I have to be the greatest. I learned to judge myself by those who accepted me. Therefore, if I analyze those ideas and convince myself they're foolish, I'll break the jealousy habit."

Isn't that hopeful? Can you see how close at hand

44

peace of mind is? How can you be discouraged with such insights? Counselors encounter persons all the time who swear they were neurotically jealous earlier in their lives but are so no longer. That doesn't surprise me, because I hear people saying the same thing about anger, which they never believed they could control (because they were redheads or Irish), or laziness (because they had seldom disciplined themselves).

Behavior can change. Jealousy is behavior. It is a habit. It can be changed if you know what causes it and if you work hard to combat it.

Smile, a new day for you is dawning.

For you to control jealousy and possessiveness it is critical that you learn what modern psychology has to say about the latest techniques available. Only by knowing how you become jealous in the first place and knowing what to do about it in the second place can you get the control it will take to give you peace of mind and patch up the hurt feelings your jealousy has caused. To do this, you must learn the ABC's of emotion. Even if you have read about the ABC Theory of Emotional Disturbance before, review this section to refresh your memory. It can't hurt you.

Basically we can experience two kinds of pain: physical and emotional. A physical pain affects the body in obvious ways: broken bones, spilled blood, bruised skin, and the like. Emotional pain is deep inside but shows none of the above signs common to physical injury.

If a man strikes you with his fist, it is correct to say that he hurt you. You didn't hurt yourself. I didn't hurt you. Your aunt Tilly didn't hurt you. That man hurt you. Your pain was caused by a fist, and there's little you can do about the pain except nurse it and let it heal in time.

But suppose that man curses you. He throws words at you instead of fists. How would you feel? Hurt? Probably. However, that's called emotional pain because nothing painful was done to your body. You wouldn't be bleeding, no bones would be broken, and no muscles bruised.

So where does your pain come from if not from the nasty language? *It comes from your own words, your thoughts, your self-talk.* If you make certain painful statements to yourself over the man's nasty remarks, *those painful statements* can give you great emotional pain, such as feelings of depression, guilt, inferiority, anger, fear, or jealousy.

Study that statement carefully. It will change your life. Thinking logically and rationally can protect you from any of those emotions every time you decide to think sensibly instead of hysterically.

Irrational Thoughts of Jealous Persons

1. *I'm no good unless someone loves me.*

Nonsense. Who, besides you, says so? If you accept yourself, you're protected when others don't accept you. Are you a child that you need to be loved? If so, what would happen to you if your partner died? Would you perish? Would you not be able to function again after a reasonable period of grieving? Of course you would. After childhood, you do not need love, even though life is beautiful when you have it.

Furthermore, how can you believe you need the love of someone when for most of your life you did not have that love? If you fell in love at age twenty-one, are we to suppose you were a miserable person for all those

46

years before that love affair? You probably had years of good times before your lover entered your life. You'll have years of good times if and when your lover rejects you.

Lastly, why do you insist on making someone else a judge of your worthwhileness? How did this one who loves you become an expert of your merits, your total value? Did your partner obtain a degree in college in how to grade human beings? I know of no such degree.

If you think this idea through carefully, you'll stop singing that neurotic song, "You're nobody till somebody loves you."

2. *You belong to me, so do as I command.*

One of the most dangerous beliefs held by jealous and possessive people is that they actually own someone once mutual love has been expressed. Should one partner decide that feelings have changed, this insanity—that one person owns another person; "We're married, so you belong to me"—rears its infantile head.

"I bought the license, I buy your food, your clothes, I pay for the house, the medical bills, I earn the money. You're mine, body and soul." So *he* says.

"I bear your children, I cook, clean, keep the house, I make a million sacrifices for you and the kids. I insist you owe me your company, your loyalty, your earnings, and your love. No other woman has a right to you." So *she* says.

No one owns anyone else, even where the law of the country allows it. Such laws are wrong and always have been. Unfortunately the concept of slavery is still much alive and may always be. It is simply too easy to believe that vows taken at a church altar are the equivalent of

47

life sentences. They are not and had better not be.

A loving relationship is nothing more nor less than an agreement between two individuals to fulfill specific conditions for that relationship to survive. It is a contract to service the deep desires and needs of each other *as long as each desires.* When either party wishes to terminate that contract, nothing should prevent it. *Marriage Is a Loving Business* is the title of my book in which I fully explain the Reciprocity Theory of Love and the Business Theory of Marriage. I make the point that marriage is similar to employment and that a person has a right to quit employment at any time desired.

No matter how much you have given to a relationship, you still have no right to demand that the other person must stay in that relationship. If you have sacrificed for years and your partner has betrayed you and wants a divorce, you have no moral right to forbid such an action. People do not have to be nice. This is not a just world and your partner does not *have* to be a decent person. If you are deceived, do not claim that because you do not deserve it, it cannot happen. Instead, come to a compromise over the frustrations causing such behavior, or give your mate a separation or divorce. Why hold on to an employee who does not want to work for you? Why insist that your mate cannot leave you when he or she has no desire to stay? It's better to be rid of such a person, better for you and better for your partner.

You question that? Then what do you have to say to someone who tells you: "If I can't have you, no one can. I'll kill you if you leave me." That's not just cute talk. That's a threat to your life.

If this is how you think, you've got a serious problem

and had better start some hard thinking. Question the idea that people can possess human beings just as they possess houses, clothes, and cars.

Question the notion that such neurotic attachments endear you to the person who wants to break away. Chances are your partner wants to leave you because you smother, possess, and rule that person like a jailer. No wonder the relationship is falling apart.

Question the notion that you *need* anyone when you have grown beyond childhood. Your mate is important to you, certainly. But it's irrational to hold that: *(a)* you'll die if you lose your lover, *(b)* you're worthless without your partner, and *(c)* you'll never find another lover.

If you question those notions, you just might begin to act like a reasonable person again whom your lover just might find attractive, and just might want to stay with.

3. *I must have what I want. Obey me because it's only right and fair.*

No, you don't have to have your way—ever. You deserve to be rewarded, of course. However, that does not mean you *have* to have fairness. For example, it's only right and proper for your spouse to appreciate your sacrifices. And it's only right and proper to expect your efforts to be appreciated. You don't flirt at parties or ignore your lover when companionship is wanted. So you feel that he or she *has* to repay you in the same way.

That's a demand, and that's neurotic. Why *should* your lover be nice just because you are? Doesn't everyone have the right to be immature and selfish? Everyone in the world has a perfect right to be wrong, stupid, inconsiderate, and imperfect. That's not a nice way to be, but people have a right to be human.

Am I suggesting that if you don't angrily resent such behavior, you have to accept inconsiderate behavior?

No, you don't need to accept such behavior. Instead of getting angry over the person's selfish behavior, calm down and *then do something firmly and rationally about the problem.*

For example, your husband answers the phone and doesn't tell you to whom he's talking. Instead of getting angry, grant him the right to be foolishly secretive and do the same in return. Or leave the room, or forget about it. Or do something else. But don't get jealously angry. That's the worst thing you could do.

The control of anger, resentment, and violence is so crucial to overcoming jealousy that I must go into full detail regarding this serious emotion. I rank this anger as the second most serious problem, self-blame being the first. If you wish to conquer this destructive feeling, you must learn these two skills well: First, accept yourself (never hate yourself for your weaknesses; forgive yourself for them, no matter how bad they are). Secondly, forgive others for their weaknesses.

Learn never to blame. Do not blame yourself and do not blame others. By self-blame I mean rejecting faults in yourself *and* also rejecting yourself totally as a human being. That leads invariably to feelings of (1) guilt, (2) inferiority, and (3) depression.

Other-blame occurs when you reject unacceptable *behavior* in others and then reject *them* as human beings. That act leads to feelings of (1) anger, (2) resentment, (3) hatred, and (4) often superiority and conceit.

When you eliminate blame, you rid yourself of all those painful emotions. Therefore, learn this lesson and learn it well. It is one of the most important pieces of psychological knowledge you can ever learn.

There are six steps in developing anger. (For a fuller explanation, see my book *Overcoming Frustration and Anger.*)

Step 1: *"I want something.* I want your total devotion. I want to be extremely important to you."

So far so good. No harm done. Wishing is healthy and pleasant.

Step 2: *"I didn't get what I wanted and am frustrated.* You don't think I'm the greatest. You enjoy others as much or more than me. I don't like this."

Again, so far so good. No anger has been created. A wish has not been satisfied, so you're left frustrated, not angry. That's been happening to you all your life, such as when it rains on a picnic, or when you don't discover treasure, or don't become a movie star.

Step 3: *"It is awful and terrible not to get what I want.* I hate it when I have competition. To lose your approval is worse than death. If I'm not the greatest in your life, I'm nothing."

This step is the critical point at which normal and healthy behavior becomes neurotic. If you did not think your frustration was a catastrophe, you wouldn't be getting upset. Think it through carefully and you'll convince yourself you do not need total approval, and that competition can actually be very good for your relationship.

Step 4: *"You shouldn't frustrate me. I must have my way.* You must not have outside interests. They could lure you away. I don't care what you want. I only care what I want."

51

Now you're becoming an impossible dictator just because you think you're right. You're acting like a baby who is confusing *wanting* something with *needing* something.

Step 5: *"You're bad for frustrating me.* If you do bad things such as kiss others, dance and laugh with others, or even have lunch with others, I'll not only reject your actions but I'll also reject you totally. You and your actions are the same."

No matter how much someone frustrates you, that person is never bad. People behave badly because they are: *(a)* deficient (and cannot learn to behave without fault), *(b)* ignorant (and have not had the opportunity to learn to behave without fault), or *(c)* disturbed (and cannot control what they have learned when they are too upset).

Step 6: *"Bad people ought to be punished.* You deserve to be beaten, scolded, and severely restricted because you are bad. Perhaps you'll improve if I treat you badly."

Violent behavior does not produce love and appreciation. We almost always hate people who are consistently unreasonable. Firmness is one thing; brutality, cruelty, or severe criticism is another. You can't expect to develop strong and stable persons after you deny them the very essentials of emotional growth.

Each time you get angry, go through this sequence and try to stop it as early as possible. Study these steps carefully after each angry episode and the day will come when you can disapprove of someone or something and do it with grace, dignity, *and* firmness.

4. *You made a fool out of me.*

This is not possible. No one can make a fool out of you unless *you* think you're a fool. If your friends laugh at you because your wife has been unfaithful, you don't have to feel like a fool. You haven't done anything wrong. How could you then be a fool? Let your wife examine her behavior and come to terms with her conscience. That's *her* problem. Remember, no one can upset you unless you *choose* to be upset.

If your husband whistles at every well-turned ankle or well-stuffed sweater, don't accuse him of making a fool of you. In the eyes of most people he's making a fool of himself. Don't get disturbed over his thoughtlessness. Ignore him, or do your own whistling, or get out of the car calmly and take a cab home. Take your own car to the party so you can change plans in midstream if necessary. Whatever you do, don't lose your cool, and don't put yourself down by thinking his behavior makes a fool out of you.

If you have deep respect for yourself, you remain invulnerable to the petty and mean acts of others.

5. *I'll never fall in love again.*

A powerful reason for letting yourself get upset when it seems that your lover is drifting away is the dread that you will be forever alone and unloved. Granted that would be most unpleasant, but would it be as bad as most people imagine? These are some of the things you'd likely be telling yourself:

"I haven't dated in years. I won't know how to make contact again. All the eligible individuals are already married. What's out there in society is just the leftovers no one else wants. How can I find another attractive mate now that I'm middle-aged? I'm no spring chicken anymore, and people only want young partners with smooth skin and nice figures."

No wonder you are scared the moment your marriage is put under a slight strain. If your future is actually so bleak, it's not unreasonable to expect a minor breakdown. But wait! Let's look at those statements more closely.

You haven't dated in years and you are out of practice. Getting back into the dating scene will be awkward perhaps, but if you give yourself time, you will devise your own style of socializing. You'll meet people at work, through friends, clubs, parties, or by accident. How it happens is not as important as that it happens. Most people who divorce are remarried within a few years. If you bear that point in mind, you'll be in less panic in the event that you lose your mate.

6. *All the eligible persons are already married.*

That may seem so, but it isn't. After all, there are about one million divorces a year in the United States. Those persons stay single only a few years on the average. Therefore, if you're out there making contacts, you'll probably meet a nice person just like yourself. Has it occurred to you that other divorced persons are probably saying the same thing and are including *you* in that group of ineligible mates?

7. *I'm not young anymore. How can I appeal to someone now that I've lost my youth and good looks?*

Up to a point you have a point. But the argument is not valid, except in the extreme case. What has happened to you over the years has also happened to others. However, if you are concerned about those extra bulges, get on an exercise program and a diet. You may find yourself trimmer and more fit than you ever were as a young adult. Get over the notion that you have to put yourself in mothballs merely because you have turned forty or fifty. I know individuals over fifty who run a mile in under seven minutes and do fifty push-ups. Some of them did not achieve those goals when they were younger.

What you lack in physical appeal, however, you probably make up for in personality traits which are far more appealing. Being older, you are probably wiser, more patient, more understanding. You are surely more sophisticated than you ever were at any time of your life. You are well traveled, better adjusted, smart in the ways of the world. You can converse about many subjects, you now laugh instead of giggle. Your tastes have matured so much that you probably couldn't enjoy a partner much younger than yourself even if you tried.

8. *I'll never meet anyone as good as my present mate.*
Oh, really? How in heaven's name do you know that? Do you have a crystal ball? Can you predict the future?

You could just as reasonably say that your next romance is going to be better than anything you have known. I can't guarantee that will happen. But aren't the chances of improving with practice and experience greater than your chances with less experience? That rule applies to most areas of behavior, why not the romantic also?

With all this going for you, you're depressed? You have more to offer another mate than you ever had before. You're a prize, a unique person, *and* you're available.

55

Imagine that you have just lost your lover to someone else. Your grief and jealousy are intense. You can't eat, sleep, or work because your mind is totally absorbed with this tragedy. Nothing gives you relief; not drinking, traveling, crying, or telling your sorrows to your best friend. You are obsessed with the thought of your humiliation, or that you will always be unloved, or that you are going crazy. Every day, many times, you think of these unhappy ideas. That's the nature of obsessive ideas.

An obsession is a thought you simply cannot shake. It may be pleasant in nature, such as when you fantasize constantly that some wish will be fulfilled. Or it can be painful in nature, such as those just described. Either type can preoccupy your thinking so completely that you don't have time to think about your grocery list, or a hundred other daily chores. Your efficiency can drop drastically, because these ideas have your brains in a viselike grip.

There are two ways to control such mental processes. The first attacks the deep irrational philosophical foundations that make you a worrier and an alarmist in the first place. Use this method first and often in order to prevent these ideas from gaining control. Some people, however, find that rather difficult. Another method which has lately come out of the field of the psychology of learning attacks the symptoms rather than the roots of the problem. I will first describe this thought-stopping technique, and later explain how one challenges the ideas in one's belief system.

Debora Phillips in her book *How to Fall out of Love* applies thought-stopping specifically to the jealous person.

Whenever you are plagued by one of these distressing thoughts, instantly say to yourself, "Stop." Say it quietly under your breath, or think it, or say it aloud if you find that works better. Then instantly think of a pleasant scene, a fond memory, or a happy fantasy. Keep thinking of that scene in some detail until you feel better, then go about your daily business. If the obsession emerges immediately thereafter, repeat this process. Do this all day, every time your thinking plagues you. Keep a daily record with paper and pencil or a golf counter. You'll notice that your totals from day to day will fluctuate wildly. Don't lose heart. Keep up this distraction technique and you will notice a marked decline over a period of two to four weeks.

Incidentally, distracting with only one pleasant thought can become boring. Prepare a half dozen distracting thoughts to lend variety to your daydreaming.

What are these distractions like? Everything from dining in a fine restaurant to riding a white horse across a green meadow on a cool spring morning in Wyoming. Or how about winning an Olympic event, or listening to the rain falling in a forest? When I ask my clients to choose a restful scene, can you guess what most appeals to them? It's vacations. Either they are driving through scenic country or they are sunning themselves on a beach. However, that is an individual matter. Choose your own pleasures. It is difficult to get upset if you are focusing on something lovely. You cannot think of something soothing or happy and something frightening at the same time.

The jealous person creates self-torment by placing the object of his or her love on a pedestal one hundred feet high. This leads to feelings of adoration and hero

57

worship. And even if these are exceptional people, they certainly don't deserve to be placed among the gods and goddesses. When they are, their loss is felt with an intensity that has to hurt.

How can you alleviate this feeling? By being honest with yourself. Be realistic. No one is perfect, no one is conceivably as beautiful or necessary as you imagine your partner to be. That is a figment of your imagination. Bring that individual down to earth, to the level of other mere mortals. Enough of this glorification of people who are not paragons, who have no blemishes, and who are never petty.

Be honest with yourself and with them. See them for *all* they are, not only their fine and admirable features. Your lover is human, and as a human shares all the faults, follies, and fallibilities of the race.

You cannot help feeling less hurt by your loss if you treat your unresponsive lover this way. If this does not work, go one step farther. Instead of just looking more at that person's negative qualities, think also of that person in a ridiculous situation.

Is your lover neat about clothes and appearance? Then imagine him or her falling face down in the mud. See your mate getting up, with mud dripping from the end of the nose and the fine clothes gooky and oozing with black slime.

Does your partner like to be the center of attention? Or does he feel overly important because he gives speeches? Or does she nag a lot and find fault with you and others? Then envision your partner getting a custard pie in the face. Funny? Of course it is. It's harmless fun because it's only in your mind.

I previously pointed out that the major difficulty jealous and possessive people have is that they distrust themselves. In any contest, whether the opponents are in-laws, friends, or even children, jealous persons are positive they will lose out in the competition. In short, they don't trust themselves to win against even the weakest opponent.

This lack of self-confidence stems from the low positive regard they have for themselves. If they could respect themselves more, they would fear others less. Lack of self-acceptance, therefore, is their major problem.

How do you learn to accept yourself regardless of your crooked nose, bent legs, bald head, buckteeth, childish temper tantrums, unsophisticated upbringing, and a hundred other faults? By separating those traits, characteristics, and peculiarities from you as a person. Just as you can reject your shoes because they have holes in the soles but not reject your feet, so you can reject things *about* you without rejecting yourself.

If you never put *yourself* down, how can you fail to have self-respect? It would be impossible, wouldn't it? Try it and see.

Let me put it another way. People who feel easily threatened and who feel guilty or inferior almost always give themselves two grades for everything they do. The first grade is for the things they have done; the second grade is for themselves as human beings. It is the second grade which creates insecurity and jealousy.

For example, if you dance poorly, you are correct to give yourself a grade of F for dancing. If you kept your child in a turmoil today with your nagging and yelling, you'd have a right to grade yourself F as a parent.

If you would now decide to improve that grade by

getting dancing lessons or learning to be more patient with your child, you'd gradually be able to raise those F grades to D's, then C's, and perhaps up to A's.

That's what you tried to do all your life while attending school. Sometimes you improved considerably, sometimes not at all. In the end you had grades that told you how good you were in reading, spelling, and math.

Most people don't leave it at that, unfortunately. They decide to grade themselves as *human beings* as well. That's when they get into trouble. For if you think you are an F person because you are an F dancer, you'll feel badly about *yourself.* If you dislike *yourself* because you don't like the way you handle your children, you'll feel guilty and inferior. It's the F's and D's you give yourself as a person that make you unsure of yourself. When you convince yourself day after day that you aren't any good (rather than just having some inferior skills), you're bound to think everyone else will consider you worthless too.

Stop this self-rating. Never judge yourself. Always judge *only* your actions whether others do so or not. Then you will never hate yourself.

Accept yourself with your faults but change them if you can. If you can't change them, accept yourself as an imperfect person who never has to be put down because of poor behavior.

"Love thy neighbor as thyself," we are constantly admonished. If most of us loved our neighbors as we love ourselves, we'd go next door right now and start a fight.

Always judge your actions but never judge yourself, good or bad. There are no good people or bad people in the world. There are only people who do good or bad things.

That's self-acceptance. And that's how you build up a self-image you can live with.

What if Your Mate Is Unfaithful?

A woman asked whether I help people who have discovered that their mate has been unfaithful. Such had happened to her and she wondered if it was "normal now to be depressed, unsure, demeaned, and feeling belittled and humiliated." She reported that she felt she had lost her self-worth and self-confidence because she had been so sure of her marriage. Her trust is gone, she thinks of getting even, feels betrayed, hurt, and jealous.

The above description is all too common. The lady is behaving quite normally, to be sure. But she is behaving in a way that is self-defeating. I advised her to be less normal but more healthy. And here is how she can do it.

First, she should not judge herself by her mate's actions. Why does she suddenly feel worthless? How has *she* changed? What has *she* done that was so wrong? He had the affair, not she. So why should she crucify herself for what *he* did?

But suppose she drove him to it? Not likely. Although she may have frustrated him throughout the years, you can be certain he frustrated her too. Surely he was unreasonable at times, cutting in his remarks, and rejecting in his behavior. Yet she did not cope with the problem as he did.

Secondly, she should not think that she is less of a person because her husband loved another woman for a time. Most people feel inferior when their loved ones have preferred someone else. But why should they? To conclude that this woman is less of a person because her husband loved someone else places him in the position of a judge over her. Yet how can he determine her value simply because he rejected her? Is he an expert on people? Who gave him authority to declare her worth?

The woman herself is the one making these judgments. She compares herself to the other woman and decides erroneously that she must be less if her husband prefers the other. If she were thinking carefully, she could as easily conclude instead that his standards have deteriorated because he prefers someone else. What proof is there that this isn't so?

Thirdly, she could regard the whole regrettable experience as a problem that requires correction. Instead of taking his behavior personally, she could decide that something is wrong with the marriage which requires attention. And, of course, such is usually the case. An affair usually occurs for one of two reasons: the person gets bored with one lover and wants a change, or the person feels sufficiently frustrated in the marriage to seek happiness elsewhere.

If the latter is the case, this woman could get to the heart of the matter quickly enough by talking to her husband and finding out why he is so unhappy. Then she could make great efforts to please him more until he feels less frustrated. That would tend to increase his feelings of love for her and perhaps speed up the exodus of his mistress.

Lastly, she could learn not to pity herself because she

is treated so shabbily. If she could avoid being angry or spiteful because of his faithlessness, she would be reducing her misery considerably. That is the goal she could wisely adopt. It would prevent an escalation of her pains and limit the problem to the infidelity only. Otherwise she would suffer pain from the frustrating husband *and* pain from her emotional disturbances (depression, anger, and jealousy) as well. Granted, it is not easy to control such feelings, but to do so affects one's health as well as one's peace of mind.

Hide Your Jealous Thoughts

One thing that jealous persons do that makes matters infinitely worse is to complain continually. It is bad enough to be so scared in your heart that you can't stand having your partner even look at a member of the opposite sex. Imagine how much worse it is to comment every time an eligible candidate comes into view.

Why couldn't she have kept silent about her suspicions? Did she have to express a feeling merely because she had one? Of course not. Every day of the week she probably has had to swallow a lot of guff from her landlord, her parents, and even her friends. If she had expressed her feelings on every occasion, she would have been thrown out of her quarters, rejected by her parents, and come up friendless.

Yet that same person who repeatedly shows admirable control with every other living person for whom she has only passing interest blurts out obscenities, accusations, and caustic comments to the one person she cares the most about. The following conversation was with an attractive but jealous young woman.

CLIENT: I'm tired of messing up my life.

THERAPIST: How so?

C: I can't have a normal relationship with a man. I have these terrible fits of jealousy. I get off on a tangent. Usually I can control it, but when I get off on a tangent, I will get to a point where I accuse men of things that are unrealistic and I know what it is going to do but I do it all the time.

T: Such as? What sort of things do you accuse them of?

C: Being with other women. Not loving me. Wanting to spend time doing other things. I suppose anything that takes attention from me, and I dwell on it. I have even been told that I look for it and try to create problems for myself. I will go through things of my boyfriend, looking for things. I won't wait to hear something bad. There may not even be something bad, but I will look for something bad.

T: What do you do then?

C: Look through telephone bills. Looking for calls to other girls. Strange phone numbers. Strange messages.

T: You mean the telephone rings, he answers it, and you are always wondering if it is another girl?

C: Yes, a lot of times.

T: What other ways do you show your insecurity?

C: I get upset if a man spends time flirting with another woman.

T: Any man?

C: My boyfriend.

T: What does he have to do before you think he is flirting?

C: It's hard to say. Talk in a manner that gets me upset.

T: He doesn't have to be holding on to her or he doesn't have to be kissing her, or dancing with her?

C: No, if she is getting more attention than me in any way, if he looks at her too much or something, then I wonder, Why isn't he looking at me?

T: How many boyfriends have you lost this way?

C: I suppose it has really been noticeable since my early twenties. When I was in high school I sort of dated one guy for two or three years until I got bored with him. When I was twenty or so I started dating others, and I have seen a pattern off and on since then.

T: What is the pattern?

C: I will date somebody, heavily at first, and eventually end up getting pretty close and pretty serious. Then in a month or so we are at a party and he does something to upset me and I lose my temper and yell at him.

T: At the party?

C: Yes, even at the party. Afterward I would confront him. Then a month after that another incident would occur and by the time six months had gone by (if a person can stand me for that long), I am driving him nuts. Once a week I may find something really bad to complain about.

The last guy I went with for almost two years and we were going to get married and I did the same thing. He told me to see somebody at that time. He said: "I don't care what happens to us. I want you to see somebody."

I have known that I should for a long time, but it

has been really hard for me to do. I have wanted to. I can remember when I was in my early twenties I really wanted to and then last night with this guy, he said, "I don't care what happens to us, if we break up it doesn't matter, but for you personally, I think it is a life-and-death matter that you get help."

T: Are you still engaged to this person?

C: We have been living together for fifteen months, and in the past couple of months, off and on. Things haven't gone exactly my way. I thought maybe I would move out and just give up on him. I don't know for sure that he is the right person for me. He has done some things that I would object to even if I could straighten myself out. But right now I know that if I move out because I am not happy, I would get involved with someone else again and would end up the same way. I am tired of this.

T: How many relationships are we talking about?

C: Maybe ten.

T: Ten since about the age of twenty? That's about one a year. Apparently these relationships looked promising for a period of time and then they all ended up the same way: you driving the men away with your jealousy and possessiveness?

C: Right. Those are the ones that I get serious about. I have dated men that I really wasn't interested in and eventually quit dating them. But the ones that I want to continue with, the ones that I am interested in, always turn out that way.

T: So, the more you care about a man, the more jealous you become, don't you?

C: Right. Even Benny, the one I am going with now. At first I really don't care that much. When I started

66

dating him, my first impression was: Why is that guy bothering me? I really don't see that much in him. But I'll go out with him. He seems nice enough. They are all attracted to me until they see that something is wrong.

Now listen to what she is saying six sessions later.

C: I really haven't had any jealousy feelings or incidents since the last time I talked to you. I don't know why, except that the things you say are beginning to make sense. Worrying about Benny and other girls just isn't that much on my mind anymore. I was with him last Friday night.

There were several girls that he was talking with and I could see that he treated them just like men, you know, just people to talk to. And I talked to people too and had a good time.

T: What did you say to yourself that made you feel less threatened when you saw him talking to other women? You would not have done that before, would you?

C: Well, it probably depends on what I would see. The last time I got jealous we were in the same place and he went to the bathroom and I got up to get my girl friend and myself a drink. I walked past him and he was talking to another girl and they were hugging. They hadn't seen each other for a while I guess. At that time I was really jealous and it really made me mad that I should get up out of my chair and find him doing something like that. But he hadn't seen the girl for a long time and they were just friends, and it was just a friendly hug and it didn't really bother me.

T: Well, was that recently?

67

C: No, that was maybe three or four weeks ago. At the time it bothered me and we kind of argued about it. And I asked him what was going on, but as I think back on it, the thought doesn't upset me at all.

T: O.K. If that had happened today, how would you have reacted?

C: Oh, I would say there's a girl he hasn't seen for a while. They're good friends. Big deal.

T: That's what you would think?

C: Yes.

T: What else would you have to say to make sure you wouldn't get all jealous?

C: I don't know, I don't find myself having to say anything right now.

T: Well, if you began to feel a little bit jealous, let's say you would, what else would you have to say to talk yourself out of it?

C: So what if he's hugging her? So what if he thinks she's attractive? Big deal. There are a lot of other attractive people in the world too.

T: I don't need this man.

C: Yeah. I'm beginning to say that.

T: Right. It's not going to kill me if he rejects me and falls in love with her.

C: True.

T: Aren't you beginning to see that?

C: Yes.

T: That wouldn't be very nice, it would be a disappointment, it would be very sad. Right?

C: Uh-huh.

T: But would it actually kill you?

C: No.

68

T: And would it mean that nobody else would ever love you?

C: No.

T: So what's the big deal?

C: Yeah.

T: Maybe sometimes he does have very positive thoughts about some of these other women. But most of the time he's probably being innocent. But there are times when he may in fact have desires for these other women and prefer them over you. That's when I want you also not to be jealous.

C: Yes.

T: That's the test. When he really does want to reject you, I want you to be able to live through rejection and to convince yourself it is not the end of the world to be rejected. You are perfectly O.K. whether he— what?

C: Loves me or not.

T: Loves you or not, right.

C: There really hasn't been anything that I've really been suspicious of lately, so maybe that's not a good test of that anyway.

T: Well, I hope you don't have such a test. But if it ever came along, that's the way to handle that kind of doubt. Don't you see?

C: Yes.

T: If he does care for her more than me, well, I'll have to live through that, that's all. I'm not worthless because of what he does. I'm not a slob. I'll live through it. I'm not a bad gal. That's what you could say to yourself, and you will then ride through any potential rejection. You can't be upset and you can't be jealous if you have those kinds of thoughts. How could you be?

Don't Take Behavior Personally

Jealous people are dressed in the garments of the paranoid personality. Their exquisite sensitivity; their tendency to project blame onto others, never onto themselves; their habit of reading much more into behavior than others do; and their overreaction to a presumed injustice, reaction that is so out of line that it becomes overkill: these are all hallmark signs of the paranoid. If that doesn't scare you, you're in serious trouble. Either way, you require much greater understanding of people, or of yourself, or both. Don't send your girl friend, or your husband, or anyone else to counseling. Go yourself, and go first. Your partner requires help too, but not nearly as much as you do. To recognize that makes you honest and mature, not devious and weak. In counseling, one of the first lessons in psychology which you would learn is that you take too many things personally.

Understand this about people: the way they behave toward you is just about the same way they behave toward others with whom they have a similar relationship.

If your friend gossips behind your back, don't get insulted. Give him time and you'll see soon enough how he also gossips about his other friends. If your wife tells you to keep your eyes riveted on the road ahead of you, have compassion for her instead of getting mad. Her ex-husband or her old boyfriends were treated the same way. You'll discover that she has a *pattern* of behavior

70

and is only doing what she usually does. When she's with you her jealousy lashes out at you. When she's with her mother, father, sister, brother, boyfriend, fiancé, or ex-husband, her jealousy lashes out at that person.

That's true of much of her other behavior. You enjoyed how friendly she was to you when you first met, didn't you? Well, that's her pattern. Expect her to be friendly to many other people too. That's the way friendly people are. They don't act that way just to make you insecure. They act that way because *that's the way they are.* They can change, of course. But for the time being, accept them with their irritating faults and try calmly and rationally to change them.

For example, if you get uptight about the friendly telephone conversations your wife often has with men she works with from the office, don't take that personally. Don't think that a hot romance is brewing. Take stock of her patterns and you will see that she talks to everyone in a friendly way.

First, tell her you don't like her chummy attitude and ask her to modify it. If that doesn't work, fight fire with fire and show her what it sounds like when you talk like that to women. If she's not threatened, all the better, because you might enjoy this pattern for yourself and want to keep it up. If you, however, deeply disapprove of such familiarity, consider her as having a neurotic problem and unable to help being a flirt or a show-off (if that's what you think she is).

Your task then is to learn to live with a neurotic. Realize that she has a bad habit and would do the same even if we could pluck you out of the relationship and put in any Tom, Dick, or Harry. Her behavior would remain the same in all likelihood. That's the way flirts are. That's the way show-offs are. If she weren't a flirt or a show-off, she wouldn't behave that way.

So, instead of taking her actions personally, expect the next phone conversation to be filled with a lot of chumminess. Expect her to be flattered by these attentions. That may be immature and silly behavior for a person her age, but then what can you expect from a lovely person who has that hang-up? Remember, you have a string of hang-ups too, the worst of which is your own neurotic tendency to turn green whenever a phone call is for her.

Listen to Your Lover

You've heard the expression, haven't you, about not being able to see the forest for the trees? That can certainly apply to the jealous lover and his or her partner.

When your lover keeps telling you how unreasonable you are to be so suspicious, don't automatically dismiss such charges. In the vast majority of cases your partner will be right and you will be wrong. Remember, your paranoid nature, your deep sense of insecurity and inferiority practically compel you to see evil intent where none exists. Still, try to put yourself in the shoes of your lover and seriously consider the charges that your imagination frequently carries away all your reason.

Friends and neighbors are often able to point out our merits and faults far more accurately than we are. They can even make judgments about our children which escape us. They are looking through eyes that are less biased than ours are.

Jealous persons are so prejudiced in their own beliefs

that they become unreliable guides by which to judge another's behavior. To question your convictions at that stage gives you one of your greatest tools for helping yourself. To admit that you might be wrong is an enormous step in the right direction. Just as a mother cannot accept her son's deserving a jail sentence because she is too controlled by her feelings, so too you are so controlled by your fears that your objectivity is almost completely lost.

Therefore, don't tell your mate how wrong he or she is when you're accused of being supersensitive. *You probably are* supersensitive.

I realize you're too scared, too dependent, you think too little of yourself to believe that you can give up your suspicions. Even so, never forget that jealousy is one of the first symptoms shown by the paranoid. And the paranoid practically always believes his or her beliefs before anyone else's. That doesn't make you right *most* of the time, only occasionally. So why not play the odds in your favor and seriously consider that your imagination is running away with your better judgment. Accept the other's opinions more often. You may find yourself getting along a great deal better if you do.

3
How to Become a Superlover

THUS FAR I HAVE WRITTEN MAINLY OF TECHNIQUES which you, a jealous person, can use *to change yourself.* By changing yourself you are likely to have a positive influence on your partner. Now, however, let us look at methods that can affect *the other person.*

Since the threat of losing your lover is always your first concern, whatever you can do to reduce that threat will make you feel better. First, however, it is essential that you understand what love is all about. Many prevailing notions about love are incorrect and unrealistic. What I am about to explain about love comes from years of thought, reading, and counseling, and every day that passes convinces me more and more that my Reciprocity Theory of Love is indeed valid (see *Marriage Is a Loving Business*).

Mind you, I don't particularly like what I discovered. I wish human nature were different. But it isn't. So put aside any poetic and romantic ideas about love that you may have and look at this subject with objectivity.

Love is that powerful feeling you have for anyone who satisfies your deepest desires and needs.

People love you when, and only when, you please

74

them. Love is a self-centered emotion. I'm referring only to love at the individual level, as encountered in romance, marriage, family, and friendships. I am not referring to the concept of love for humankind, or that which urges us to be our brother's keeper. That does not require reciprocity. When you send a CARE package to a starving family in a foreign nation, you don't know or particularly care who gets it. And you don't expect a gift in return. It's purely an act of generosity and it's beautiful.

Intimate love, on the other hand, always expects payment in return. Each of us has deep desires and needs, and if those deep desires and needs are not satisfied to a reasonable degree, we fall out of love. It's that simple. The idea that you ought not to place any conditions on love is noble, but it doesn't work. It doesn't conform to reality. If you do not require appreciation for your efforts, you are either *(a)* a saint or *(b)* a neurotic. Most people are *not saints.*

If you are neurotic, it is because you allow yourself to be treated badly, you tolerate abuse. You show little concern for yourself, and you train your mate to be so selfish that he or she becomes impossible to live with.

In all the years I have counseled people I have never met one person who fell out of love because his or her partner was perfect. There is always a long list of complaints one person has about the other. I find that the strained feelings can be relieved if I can get the rejected party to understand what the frustrations are in his or her lover, and to remove them. If love is not totally dead, this method will usually revive the flickering flame.

This point is crucial for you, the jealous person, to

understand. When you feel your lover is losing interest, don't deny him or her those things that are deeply desired and needed. That's what you do when you attack, become too possessive, or show how insecure you are. Your partner didn't marry you to be criticized all day. He or she expected to be made happy and to have fun living with you.

So, if your husband wants a cleaner house, clean it. He'll love you for it. If your wife wants to socialize more, let her. It will strengthen your marriage. If he likes to dance with every woman in the place, let him. You'll make more points that way than you will if you have a scene.

Look at it this way: we don't love people directly, we love what they do for us. We love their acts, not them.

But what if he wants to have an affair? Do you let him do that and still expect more love? Of course not. There is a point beyond which you do not want to go to please anyone. It's called the point of Just Reasonable Contentment.

Let's suppose it takes one thousand calories to keep you just on the verge of health. You use one thousand calories a day, but you replace them with another one thousand calories every day.

Now suppose you used one thousand calories a day but were able to replace those with only nine hundred a day. In thirty-five days you would be lacking three thousand five hundred calories and that would be a loss of one pound. At that rate you'd be a skeleton in a few years and you'd be at the starvation level.

Just as it takes calories, among other things, to stay physically healthy, so too it takes emotional food to stay psychologically healthy and contented. These emo-

76

tional victuals are called strokes. A stroke is a touch on the arm, a pat on the cheek, a hand on the shoulder, a kiss, a smile, a compliment, a favor, a gift.

Let us say it takes ten strokes a day to make you just reasonably content emotionally. But suppose that repeatedly you receive nine. The one you may want the most is attention from your mate. You want to feel important, and when you're ignored you feel psychologically hungry. If that condition continues for weeks or months on end, the day will come when you are so starved emotionally that you won't even be able to say to yourself that you are *just reasonably content.*

That's a dangerous time in any relationship. If you remain below the JRC level too long, three conditions result almost without fail. First, you become distressed and unhappy because you feel continually frustrated. Secondly, you'll begin to fall out of love with your mate. And, thirdly, you'll fall out of love with the relationship.

This information is vital for the jealous person to digest. It means, purely and simply, that when you are unhappy with your mate, don't push for too much change or you'll lose that person totally.

If you forbid your lover to dance with anyone but you, the total satisfactions within the relationship are going to diminish somewhat. If you insist he cannot have a beer with the boys, or she cannot have lunch with the girls, the total rewards of living with you get still lower.

Be careful, or soon you may have your partner below the JRC point where he or she will get disturbed, love you less, and love the marriage less.

But what if you're still not happy yourself? You've pressured your partner for changes and they have been made. You want more but you know that will bring on more friction. So what do you do?

When the other person has to become miserable to make you happy, back off if you can and resign yourself to getting less than you had hoped. Or if you are miserable because you aren't just reasonably content, consider separation or divorce.

The jealous person had better realize that one can push only so much before rejection and hate begin to replace love. If you truly want your lover to stay with you, to be able to say: "I'm reasonably content, I like being close to you, I don't mind this too much, I'm glad we married," then give that person satisfaction each day. Otherwise, you and that relationship are in serious trouble.

All people who marry, but especially the jealous and possessive ones, seem to have little idea of what marriage truly is. They think it is an arrangement made in heaven and that once the ring is slipped on the finger an invisible ring is also slipped through the nose. The idea that you belong to each other and that you will stay wedded in sickness and in health is a truly fine sentiment, but not one all people take seriously.

If you understood the realistic basis for marriage, you would never consider marriage a state that has to last forever. Jealous people would just love to have their mates think so because they then could do what they pleased and get away with it.

One of the worst tyrants I ever encountered was a man so jealous his wife couldn't even talk to the neighbor except to say hello. If someone complimented her, even in the most innocent way, he would harass her so hard she would avoid that person again. And he was totally against divorce. I could easily understand why.

As long as she believed that she was his property because she once said "I do," he could hound her as much as he liked and didn't worry about it a bit. He never seemed to understand that marriage is very much like a business.

His wife felt, before she married him, that she'd be happier with him than without him. So she married the man fully expecting a reasonably happy existence. When he became insanely jealous of her, she lost her feelings of love because he wasn't satisfying her deep desires and needs *to a reasonable degree.* Still she felt she had to put up with it *because she was married.*

In my view, any married person always has the option of leaving a marriage just as a person is always free to leave a distasteful job.

Suppose you worked at a job at which you expected specific benefits and didn't get them. Would you feel guilty about quitting that job? Of course not. Well, why is marriage so much different? When your mate makes you miserable over the years, pressure him or her to change, but if no change occurs, think of firing your mate just as you would an employee. For that's what we are: partners in a business called Smith & Smith or whatever. As long as the partnership makes both of you reasonably content, stay with it. When it turns sour, quit, sell your interest in the business, and start over elsewhere.

How is marriage any different? Last year one million couples divorced for precisely these reasons. Jealous persons must learn that their partners have every right to fire them in the same way that any boss has a right to fire any employee. That may sound a bit harsh, but that's the way things are.

The success of a business is measured by its profits. The success of a marriage is measured by the happiness it produces. If your insecurity is so great that your mate is not happy with you, watch out that you don't press too hard or your dreams will end in divorce. You are the ones this happens to more often than to others. Your lack of understanding of how a mate and an employee are similar is your great weakness.

You have only four choices before you when dealing with unacceptable behavior in your family, job, friendship, or marriage. The first three are rational and healthy choices. The fourth is the only one I don't advise. If you want to be a superlover, realize that your mate has these options just as you do and that you will be sorely hurt if you force him or her to use certain options, especially the second and third, and somewhat the fourth.

Option No. 1 is *Toleration Without Resentment.* Our maturity and common sense tell us we don't need to be alarmed over every disappointment. If you have a tendency toward jealousy, I would strongly advise this option most of all. Tolerate those phone calls your wife has from her friends. Tolerate his lunches with the saleswomen he meets in the business world. Tolerate her demonstrative ways when she meets your male friends and kisses them politely. Tolerate his strong urge to look at other women or at girlie magazines. Convince yourself that these are not truly threatening to you. Even if they turn out to create a lovers' triangle, you're still better off being a pleasant but firm person about this than being an unpleasant but firm person.

The crux of the argument for choosing Option No. 1 is that most of the events we fear simply never happen.

How much wiser and easier it is to resign ourselves to an issue that is not very important.

A young man I'll call Mark had been deeply in love with one girl for several years. After high school she went off to college and he into a downtown business. At first their letters were fairly frequent, but as the months passed they became fewer. She was interested in some-one else.

At first he was beside himself with jealousy. He was depressed, angry, and scared of being alone. Calling her nightly was his first solution. Visiting her on weekends was his second. Seeking her pity was his third. That's when he came for advice.

I asked him to examine why he felt so disturbed. Naturally he insisted it was her rejection of him. I refused that interpretation, because it was he who upset himself.

Instead, I told him to sit tight, not to make too much out of her current romance, and to live through a rejec-tion if it happened. I also reassured him that by being mature and calm about things he could gain the respect of his girl friend, and maybe her love. Perhaps she had to experiment a bit. That could be healthy.

So he relaxed, showed her attentions for the next six months, and eventually won her back. Option No. 1 did the job.

Suppose your lover's behavior is so annoying that total toleration is out of the question. What then? My advice is to switch from submissiveness to assertiveness. Refuse to give in another inch until some concession is made to you. Unless you do so, your level of content-ment will drop below a healthy point and you'll become disturbed, you'll fall ever so slightly out of love with your partner, and your feelings for the relationship itself will diminish.

"How firm do you recommend I get in seeking justice?" you may be asking.

My advice is to push as hard and as long as it takes, or as hard and as long as you have strength for. If you stick to your guns, you may be rewarded with benefits and kindnesses that will make a world of difference to your happiness. If you can't hold out for all your wishes, hold out for whatever compromise you can. Any gain is usually better than none. In addition, your refusal to knuckle under will prove very helpful in the long run toward training your lover how to treat you.

I call Option No. 2 *The Strike, or the Cold War.* And I think those are accurate terms for what goes on. They are names for sound and healthy tactics to make marriage work. They often repair failing marriages or romances because they correct serious imbalances in frustrations between the parties.

"What if I pressure my mate to make certain changes and I get absolutely nowhere? In fact, what if things get worse? What should I do then?" are questions often asked.

Things almost always get more tense when you stop being the pushover. No one likes to give up ways of behaving that have been pleasing and satisfying. Change often comes about only because one partner is given an ultimatum or a threat.

Don't let that scare you. Remember, you're unhappy already. Being more miserable for a while is simply the price you may have to pay to correct the faults in your romance. Let me urge you to weather the storm and fight for your rights until your expectations are met *to a reasonable degree.*

Therefore, become stouthearted and resolve not to do favors until you receive some. Do anything you consider ethical. Don't be cooperative. Be nice, be calm, but don't give in. Agree with all the arguments, but don't give in. Listen calmly to all the attempts to make you feel guilty, but don't give in. Let yourself be accused of being crazy, but don't give in. If you value your health, your love for your mate, and if you care for your family, don't give in. Unless you get your level of contentment raised to a reasonable degree, not only do you continue to suffer but so does your partner and the children. An unhappy wife or husband is not good in any relationship. Resist the temptation for temporary relief or you will all be miserable in the long run.

"Are you really serious?" you ask.

You bet I am. Workers the world over go on strike all the time for improved conditions. Striking is an accepted and well-respected practice among discontented parties. It has improved workers' lives for years. It can do the same for lovers.

Unconditional Love

The notion has been passed down for generations, from parents to children, that the best way to preserve a relationship, such as a marriage, is to love the other person unconditionally. No matter what he or she does, no matter how sloppy the house gets, and no matter how many times he smashes up the furniture, such behavior will stop if you only show that person enough love—so the belief goes.

Many people of strong faith believe in the wonders of

self-denial and love without expectation of return. To go the extra mile; to give until it hurts, and then give more; to be absolutely loving and accepting of all aggressions—this calls for nothing short of saintly endurance. If you do not have the stamina for unconditional love, do not feel guilty for your shortcomings. Contrary to some views, I do not believe that type of love is all that desirable anyway.

Unconditional love serves its high purpose only when it is offered to persons who can profit from that sacrifice: infants and *mature* adults. These are the only ones who do not usually abuse the generosity and kindness shown them. The infant cannot play mind games, the mature adult seldom does.

A husband who helps his wife clean up the house may be returning her neglect with an act of love. If he does this every weekend for a month, she, if she is mature (and could do those chores at other times), could treasure his thoughtfulness and come to realize how kind he had been. Her love for him would increase and, to please him, she might get her chores done at other times so they could enjoy the weekend together.

Let's suppose, however, that she begins to take his help for granted. She loves what he has done and thinks he's a great mate. Later she accepts his help with the laundry, then with dishes, and so on. That's abuse. She's taking advantage of his kind services. His unconditional love isn't helping him or her, is it?

If a woman jumps every time her husband yells and she hopes thereby to make her marriage stronger by so doing, all she succeeds in accomplishing is teaching him to yell again. The mature man, however, would say: "I'm sorry I yelled at you, honey. Thanks for doing me

that favor anyway, but, hereafter, let me help you too."
The immature man rationalizes that he had a right to
his request and that she has no right to complain.

By loving unconditionally you reward your partner
for mature or immature behavior, depending on which
type you are getting. That will never work for long for
the average person. The worse one partner becomes,
the more decent the other is in return. How is the
partner to know which actions are unacceptable? By
your politely mentioning it? But that's my point. Only
mature people can see the error of their ways by being
gently pressured into change. Selfish people need to be
confronted with views other than their own. And when
you present views forcefully, you are not being unconditionally loving.

If you truly care, don't let your mate become a selfish
and inconsiderate person. By putting specific conditions on your love you teach that person to give as well
as to receive. "Love thy neighbor as thyself." Remember? The totally tolerant person cares only for the welfare of others.

Just as you would discipline a child to make the child
behave better, so I would advise you to discipline the
adult who is emotionally immature to be respectful for
the deep desires and needs of others. In the end you will
be happier and have more self-respect, and your partner will have grown more toward being the kind of
person whom you can love.

Believe it or not, Option No. 2 saves many more marriages and prevents many more nervous breakdowns
than not using it does.

One caution: Before getting tough with your lover,
make sure you have been nice first, for a month at least.

85

The more difficult your partner is, the more loving you can be. This strategy can turn very unreasonable people into cooperative ones.

However, if this does not work, then put on the pressure and get difficult. Do not love unconditionally unless you want to feel like you've been run over by a truck.

Separation or Divorce

Option No. 3 is *Separation or Divorce*. If you cannot tolerate your lover's behavior without resentment (Option No. 1), and you have tried putting on great pressure to bring a halt to that behavior and it has not worked (Option No. 2), you may want to try Option No. 3: separation or divorce.

After putting up with her reckless spending for years, you have doubtless thought of avoiding those headaches by obtaining a separation or divorce.

After tolerating his poor work history for years, you have doubtless thought of avoiding those headaches by obtaining a separation or divorce.

People seldom take these steps casually. I never recommend this option until the first two options have been exhausted. Then, and only then, does this become a proper choice. In this respect marriage counselors differ. Some urge the marriage partners to stay together no matter what. You could be getting the third degree every other day of your life and slowly go crazy and some counselors would advise you to put up with your mate's jealous rages and accusations forever because you said you would do so in your wedding vows. That's why so many people who consider Option No. 3 don't take it. They feel guilty for going back on their word. I don't think they would be doing that.

When you vow that you will love your mate in sickness and in health you normally have *some* reservations (even though they may never have been expressed) which would cancel those promises. You might be perfectly agreeable to nursing your mate who lost a leg, became partially paralyzed, or developed periodic emotional problems. Would you also include a nightly quarrel, a monthly beating, infidelity, abuse of the children, chronic gambling that keeps you on the verge of poverty, incest, or venereal disease?

Any thinking person puts a silent limit on what he or she would tolerate from the partner. It's always advisable to specify before the marriage what those limits will be. However, whether talked about or not, they are there. Practically never does a person truly believe there are absolutely no conditions at all that could not be tolerated.

Separation or divorce can be healthy moves if and when they seem necessary. It is hoped that the unreasonable mate will be taught to be more reasonable in the future. Sometimes it takes two or three divorces before that person wakes up, just as some persons finally learn how to get along at work after being fired a half dozen times. The wife or husband seeking separation or divorce is usually depressed and lonely for a time but feels much better when the total picture is considered.

Separation has two special advantages over a divorce. First, it provides both parties ample opportunity to learn what a divorce is going to be like. It can spur them into greater efforts at compromise. I have seen a number of marriages improve considerably after a period of separation of at least several months. In one case a man left his family, much to the amazement of his wife. They saw each other periodically, dined together, talked, and watched to see whether important changes were being made. When improvement was great enough they agreed to live together again under new rules.

The second advantage: separation allows for negotiation, discussion, and rehearsal without a formal breakup. Expenses are less and the emotional impact on the whole family is also less. Divorce is like major surgery for the removal of a limb. Separation is like major surgery which saves the limb. And that's a major difference. As painful as it may be, Option No. 3 is better than Option No. 4.

Toleration with Resentment

Option No. 4, *Toleration With Resentment,* is the one I advise people not to take. It is better to (1) tolerate without bitterness if you can, or (2) create pressure on your partner until important changes are achieved, or (3) separate or divorce. Those make sense and may eventually reduce tension or lead to an improvement in the relationship. But Option No. 4 is the exception. Never choose that option in your dealings in human affairs.

When you tolerate a situation with resentment, you hurt yourself. That's not serious if it's done for brief periods of time. But tolerated for months—that's a different story.

You do no one any good whatsoever if you tolerate a bad scene for a long time and get neurotic in the process. It becomes a no-win proposition.

When you tolerate frustrations *but feel resentful,* you are turning the anger inward. Numerous problems develop when you want to assert yourself but won't: sleep disturbances, eating disturbances (weight loss or weight gain), irritability, anger, outbursts, depression, headaches, ulcers, skin disorders, lowered sex drive, and spiteful behavior—all are common outcomes of suppressing the resentment.

The longer this goes on, the more the marriage suffers. Though one of you may feel that things are going great, you will little realize how much emotional acid is eating away at the once good feelings that existed in the frustrated partner. The winner in this situation is actually losing at a rapid clip. It may appear as though you have improved things, but the pressure cooker is still building up steam. When the explosion will occur is anyone's guess. But erupt it will.

Instead of allowing your love to die by temporarily pleasing your partner while you smolder neurotically, take Option No. 1 or Option No. 2.

If it's Option No. 1, you will convert Toleration With Resentment to Toleration Without Resentment. That's an enormous improvement, but it requires skills in learning how to talk yourself out of being upset. However, even if you did succeed in not being angry over the unfairness in the relationship, you might still not want to tolerate the frustration because it is nevertheless unpleasant or annoying.

Then switch to Option No. 2 (Strike). That will immediately make things worse, sometimes greatly worse. It is a self-limiting technique, however. It burns itself out and turns into either Toleration Without Resentment (Option No. 1) or Separation or Divorce (Option

No. 3). If you're not careful, you could slip back to Toleration With Resentment (Option No. 4). If you do that, you set the merry-go-round in motion again: you hurt, the children suffer, and the partner eventually deals with a disturbed or sick human being who feels cheated, hurt, and increasingly out of love.

When you contemplate those results, who, in his or her right mind, would make that choice?

The following interview demonstrates quite clearly what happens when you stay in a frustrating relationship that won't change. The client, an attractive woman in her late thirties, felt betrayed, used, hurt, and depressed but kept fighting a losing battle. She would have been much better off to find a new friend, but instead she persisted in putting up with the present one's deception and lies, all the while becoming increasingly upset. She is a typical example of someone using Option No. 4.

THERAPIST: How long has this relationship been going on?

CLIENT: Four years.

T: And did you love this man?

C: Unfortunately I am afraid I do and should not.

T: Is he married or single?

C: He is single. I needed someone to talk to and be with, and at one time he needed me. I have no one now. That is a bitter pill to swallow. I guess that is why I came to you. I can talk to you and you can't say anything. I could not talk with my girl friends no matter how close I am to them. If I ever became close to another man, I would. I just would not share this

90

with friends. I have seen too much of that and it is bad.

T: Good idea. When did you find out that he was having another relationship? Let's give him a first name.

C: Call him Jake. I found out about a year ago.

T: That is when you first found out he was seeing someone else?

C: Right, and I persisted in seeing him. That is the bitter pill: that I needed him so badly I was willing to believe him when I should have seen. . . . He was not willing to give me the proof I desired to show me that I was important or more important than she. I just had to come to the logical conclusion that I was not as important as she was. Whether there was anything going on or not is beside the point. I, of course, imagined there was.

T: When you imagined that he was seeing her, how did you react to him?

C: It made barriers and I became much colder and it was difficult for me to communicate. I didn't feel that I could be myself naturally. Once this depression started, I lost my joy in daily events and couldn't smile at anything I normally smile at. I feel very bad about this. My darling little girl has not been given a real smile. I am so afraid she will perceive this. Not that she could understand or anything. It makes me angry, too. Life is so short not to enjoy it as fully as I could.

T: You said that he made a fool out of you.

C: This is how I felt, that he made a very big fool of me.

T: Explain that.

C: I was dumb enough to keep believing that he cared. I said, "O.K., you do these things and everything will be normal and natural again." He would always welsh in some manner. Then I would set up some more standards and we would begin again. I would say I was not going to talk to him anymore, I was not going to see him anymore. Then I would. Once I am near him my reasoning is not as good. I am comfortable when I am with him and relaxed, but when he is gone it is all back, and it never used to be that way.

T: What do you say to yourself when you think of his being with another woman? How do you upset yourself?

C: I upset myself by imagining what they are doing together, that they are sharing things together, that they are talking, and that they are enjoying life. And that I am not. I am not doing anything except sitting there suffering.

T: While you were feeling jealous, were you also feeling inferior?

C: Extremely. I feel that I have been completely demoralized because of this. I think I have always had feelings of insecurity for many, many reasons and now they are exaggerated. What are the reasons for my feeling insecure? My age. I am having a crisis there, with the wrinkles coming on and not having the kind of body or nose you want. Not having the clothes or the house you want. That makes you feel inferior because if you had planned your life you would be making more money, you could do this or you could do that. Those kinds of things make me feel inferior.

92

T: Do you realize that your feelings of inferiority are the things that are making you jealous?

C: Very likely.

T: How do you see that?

C: I look at that other woman and she has some skills that I don't have and maybe I could develop if I would discipline myself. I think she is prettier than I am, you know—body, face, whatever—and that makes me feel inferior and that maybe she is more exciting. I don't know, but I feel very much in doubt.

T: What do you want from him now?

C: I'd like a miracle—for him to say there was nothing there. But then I don't know if I could ever believe that. He would have to show me that he cared for me.

T: You want some demonstration of deep, lasting affection and caring for you?

C: Yes, and I don't think I will get that.

T: What emotions are you most plagued by? Anger, depression, fear?

C: All of them. I don't know which one stands out the most.

The Backlash

Marriage counseling has taught me a great deal about human behavior. There was one situation, however, which I saw repeatedly and did not understand for a long time.

It is my belief that love is that strong feeling which people have for others who (a) have satisfied, (b) are satisfying, or (c) will satisfy their deep desires and needs. When deep desires go unsatisfied for a stressful period of time, the marriage develops strains. To re-

93

duce these strains I analyze what those needs are that are seeking fulfillment and show the partners how they can satisfy each other better.

According to my theory, a person falling out of love whose needs are again satisfied ought to feel loving once more. But such was often not the case. Often persons who were being satisfied as I prescribed did not respond with immediate warmth and gratitude. They became more distant, more angry, and less loving.

I was baffled by this, and so were my clients. When I finally understood this phenomenon, I called it the Backlash. It is created for the following reasons:

1. When trying to make up with you, your mate mellows somewhat, and it is naturally easier for you to register feelings of anger and resentment at that time. You have bottled up hate and bitterness, and these emotions must be drained off before you can allow yourself to feel loving again. This process takes days, weeks, or months, depending on how intense the anger is. The sooner you talk yourself out of feeling resentful, or the sooner you ventilate those feelings, the sooner you get rid of them.

2. You may find yourself becoming angry because your mate changed after one or several talks with the marriage counselor. That can be a bitter experience. You have screamed at your partner for years. You have pleaded, cried, protested, and nothing worked. Then, following talks with a counselor, your partner comprehends your concerns and makes significant changes almost overnight. Small wonder you feel frustrated, even though you appreciate the changes.

3. While you were living in a condition of considerable frustration for all those months or years, you probably developed fantasies of what you would do after the

divorce. Or you fantasied whom you would go with. You were beginning to plan a new life for yourself and now you have to give up all those plans. This is clearly another logical reason for annoyance and resentment. Though you may enjoy the revival of your marriage, it comes at the cost of losing a future that might have had great satisfaction for you.

There you have the backlash. Accept it when you are trying to repair your love relationship. It can last for months. Let it run its course. Don't fight it. Your warmest overtures will continue to be repaid with verbal attacks, emotional coldness, and complaints of long-forgotten thoughtless acts.

Be patient. I suggest you keep this program up for three to six months. If your lover has an ounce of feeling left, that much time ought to revive those few embers of affection to a normal flame. If three to six months of satisfying deep desires and needs does not revive feelings of love again, then and only then can we be sure that the love is almost certainly dead.

The Win/Lose Outcome

You'll never be a superlover if you insist on getting your way at any cost. No one normally loves a person who is greedy, inconsiderate, and spoiled. That's what you become when you won't compromise and when you insist on getting your way far beyond what is needed to make you *reasonably content.*

Those last two words are the key to your understanding of how much pressure you want to apply in order to win. Winning is extremely important. That's not in question. I believe everyone prefers to win to be healthy and happy. As I've mentioned already, total victory for you usually means defeat for someone else. If you can convince her there is enough money in your budget to buy a boat, well and good. If you get agreement only after you have hammered away at the subject for weeks, that's total victory for you but a strong defeat for the partner. Ultimately it will turn into a defeat for you too.

If you honestly feel that the boat is not a life-and-death matter, why not apply reasonable pressure to see if the suggestion will be accepted? But if it isn't, drop it. Otherwise you're stepping beyond what is reasonable.

How do you know when your request is reasonable or unreasonable? By the way you feel about it. If the thought of not getting your boat proves highly distressing, then stick to your guns and don't give in. If you do that often and eventually lose the love of those you are always pressuring, you'll soon learn to be less demanding. What you then regard as reasonable will change to a more mature level. Life will give you the feedback you need to monitor your errors. But if you push and push and push because you are positive you're right, and you're not making compromises to speak of, look out! You'll be heading for a fall.

Suppose a man insists he has the right to forbid his wife the freedom to attend adult education classes. She protests but he subdues her by claiming she would be neglecting the children. He wins. She loses.

Then he forbids her to work for a political party and after the evening meetings to join the group in a cocktail lounge until 11 or 12 P.M. She protests but he becomes so irate she capitulates. Again he wins. She loses.

96

He doesn't like how demonstrative she is socially. She touches and kisses in the friendly way so common today. Repeatedly he accuses her of wanting to make him jealous and insists that she act more formally. She fights back but gives in after he comes home drunk and argues until 3 A.M. He wins. She loses.

She wants a car in her name. She has a job and contributes to the family income. Even if she didn't, she'd still want a car in her name. She's wanted that for years. He doesn't want to lose control, to give her too much freedom. The tighter he can pull the reins the more comfortable he is. So again he demands his way to a point he thinks is reasonable. Again he wins. She loses.

It doesn't take a genius to figure out that this winner is eventually going to lose his mate's love and see his marriage go down the drain. He'll be wiser and sadder for his many victories and then (with her or with another mate) he may become more reasonable by lowering his expectations and allowing his mate to be just reasonably content also.

The best thing you can do to become superlovers is to win if you can, but to make sure your mate wins too. You're not going to drive anyone into the arms of another by being fair. Forget the cologne, the flashy car, the fancy dance steps. Sure they're important. Being fair, understanding, and considerate doesn't cost a thing and works a thousand times better.

Emotional Blackmail

Closely related to the strategy of win/lose is emotional blackmail. By using this technique you can easily achieve a win/lose outcome and think you have thereby strengthened the relationship. But again, the cost of winning is too much and eventually backfires. Why shouldn't it? Stop for a moment and study the following typical examples of emotional blackmail and then ask yourself how *you* would feel if someone treated you with these blackmail tactics.

EXAMPLE: Alice resents the attention that Brad gives to the children. She doesn't mind it as long as she is getting her way and has enough attention paid to her. He likes playing with children, even those not his own. She loves him deeply but, when not getting enough satisfaction, applies pressures that figuratively hit below the belt; she takes her frustrations out on her children. Suddenly she'll get tough with them and put them to bed early for the flimsiest of reasons. Often she'll yell or strike a child for behaviors she usually ignores. And then she turns on her mate, accuses him of dumping all the work on her and of being unfair because she "never gets any relief."

The message gets through loud and clear: notice her more or the children will get the brunt of her moods. That's emotional blackmail. He's in a fix and he knows it. If he pleases himself and the children, they win and she loses. If he concentrates on her, he and the children lose and she wins. Down deep he'll resent this, because he feels she's hitting below the belt. Her possessiveness is still distasteful to him and reduces his love feelings for her ever so slightly each time she forces him into that position. In time she could win battle after battle but lose the war. That's no way to be a superlover.

EXAMPLE: Floyd resents his wife's domestic expectation. She wants him home more so that their home can be a warm gathering place for the family. He wants to socialize with his friends at the golf course and to drink with them after the game. In the fall he goes hunting on as many weekends as he can manage.

Her protests irk him. When he wants to shut her up he tells her he's going out, and will come home late and drunk. After that happens a few times she learns to detect the warning signs of an impending rebellion and backs off. She knows she is being blackmailed by being accused of making him upset enough to drink. His tactic works and he wins round after round. But he too lost in the end, because she lost respect for him and they divorced. That's no way to be a superlover.

You'll seldom mend your relationship if you get moody, angry, or threaten suicide. People instinctively know when they are being manipulated. You may actually be able to convince your partner that he or she is making you behave so emotionally, but sooner or later that won't matter. Your partner may conclude that he or she is not able to make you happy and wants to leave you on those grounds. Or your partner may see through your selfish motives and fall out of love for those reasons.

To be a lover, be fun to be with. Make living with you something easy and pleasant. Don't control your mate with guilt, clever arguments, phony heart attacks, or force. If you do, you'll get your way a lot of the time and that will satisfy you. In the end, however, you will be looked upon as a difficult person, an unreasonable person, a selfish person who doesn't care what he or she has to do to be pleased.

Beware that you don't protest so much that you destroy the relationship, unless what you're protesting is of such great importance that a separation or a divorce is an acceptable alternative. If these options are acceptable, then fight for what you want. If the issue is not that important, give in with a smile. Why start a war? Be a lover, not a fighter.

Love Needs Time

Surprising as it may seem, I have a great deal of clinical evidence to prove that love needs time. Without it, love withers just as a flower wilts if not watered.

This should come as no surprise to us when we all recall how we felt during our courtship days. Lovers cherish each other's company. They walk hand in hand, strolling leisurely, talking about private matters. They attend movies together, keep the phone occupied for long stretches of time, and often resent others who invade that privacy.

That seems to be what lovers need: time to know and explore each other. Without that time people can only become acquaintances, never loving intimates. The time two persons spend together is like glue. It is the history they have between them that fights and defeats mistresses, triangles, and divorce. Small wonder its absence is such a common cause of marital unhappiness. Watch out for the intrusion of elements that keep you apart. If you do not see enough of each other, you will also not think enough of each other. "Out of sight, out of mind" is a more accurate observation, it seems to me, than "Absence makes the heart grow fonder."

How is that important time ingredient destroyed? The job or the career plans of the husband can easily destroy his marriage. If he works eight hours a day, then pores over his papers every night, what can his wife

100

have of him—his tired body at 10 P.M.? Who needs it?

Young husbands are especially prone to this danger. To get their careers moving, they usually put in long hours. Junior executives are expected to work whatever number of hours it takes to do the job. I know junior executives who worked as much as eighteen hours a day for days in a row. Can you imagine what that does to one's love life? Anger and jealousy of a mate's being married to a career are the least of the stormy emotions likely to arise.

Those men who are workaholics or who want to be president of the corporation should tell their fiancée about their work plans before they marry. She has a right to know what to expect. If she is looking for a mate who will be home for supper every night, she'd better cancel her wedding plans.

Children are a second source of interference with the time two persons need to nourish their romance. The more children a couple have, the more time they lose. As wonderful as children are, they require a great deal of attention. Sensitive and jealous mates can resent the partner who gives more attention to the children than to the spouse.

To avert these problems, regulate the number of children you will have. Plan your family well and try not to have more children than the lowest figure offered by you or your partner.

Then, too, take time out for each other. Put the children to bed early some nights so the two of you can cook steaks and have wine by candlelight. Such moments are precious and help you charge up the love feelings.

Different work shifts are a particularly difficult problem for one's love life. A woman who works on the first

101

shift, and a husband who works on the second have no time together except on weekends. When she comes home, he leaves. They practically have time only to kiss in the doorway as she comes and he goes.

Whether it be the job, children, work shift, or other factors such as hobbies, drinking with the boys, golf, tennis, gardening, watch your step that these activities don't separate you. Sometimes that temporary separation can change into a permanent one.

4
Coping with Jealous and Possessive Persons

WE COME NOW TO A MOST IMPORTANT ISSUE: HOW TO deal with the jealous person. This is not easy, as those who live with these people well know. In my opinion they are among the most difficult to live with because: *(a)* they are so frightened or angry they cannot be reasoned with, *(b)* they feel they are positively right practically all of the time, and *(c)* they deny personal responsibility for their disturbances and insist that others who are supposedly at fault must do the changing. When you have that combination working against you, you need help.

Don't Tolerate the Third Degree

The very first piece of advice I wish to offer is this: do not endlessly answer all the questions your jealous partner throws at you. If you do, you'll encourage the practice to continue every time you come home an hour late from work. Your silence is certain to cause a scene, but endure it anyway. Every time you acknowledge one question you encourage another.

"Why are you an hour late?"

"I was held up on the bridge."

"What happened?"

"I don't know, I couldn't see."

"Was it a wreck or road repair?"

"I really don't know. The fellow in the car ahead didn't have any idea either."

"What fellow?"

You see how it goes? You can't satisfy the jealous mind. Bring in one fact you didn't mention before and you're in for a *fourth* degree. Or change one item of your story from the previous recital and that computer-like brain of the jealous person will point out your inconsistency and trap you again.

Your refusal to answer questions of a suspicious nature will actually help the suspicion to increase. Your partner's reasoning will be something like this: "If you have nothing to hide, why won't you answer? A clear conscience wouldn't be evasive. If you don't answer my innocent questions, you *must* have something to hide."

If your partner doesn't just think such thoughts but expresses them out loud, pay no attention. Refuse to acknowledge the question, because it deserves no answer, just as you would not answer any other absurd question.

Suppose your partner asked you quite seriously, "Did you kill Abraham Lincoln?" Surely you wouldn't, even for a moment, consider the question as worthy of serious answer, would you?

Instead of defending yourself endlessly against absurd accusations, try to train your partner out of asking such questions. The best way to do that is to offer a civil answer once or twice and then offer no more.

"I had to stop off at the drugstore, honey. It took me longer than I thought."

"It shouldn't have taken you an hour. Picking up a roll of film takes five minutes."

"True. But you know how it is, what with traffic, parking, and so on."

"It still shouldn't have taken an hour."

O.K., you've answered twice. It's not getting you anywhere. Don't continue to defend yourself. Do one of two things: shut up, or focus on the jealousy. If you choose to remain silent, your partner may become incensed and double the questioning. Remain silent. If there are threats of violence, divorce, emotional blackmail, remain silent. That won't be easy for the moment, but if you adhere to that policy, you may be rewarded in a matter of weeks by a partner who has so little faith in the third degree that it will be given up. Remember: behavior you do not reward becomes extinguished. The only reason the third degree has been used on you so long is that you have rewarded your partner by answering all the questions thrown at you. Ironically, you have wanted the grilling to cease but you actually encouraged *more* questions. If you do not want that, then keep quiet.

Or, you can focus on the jealousy. Respond to make him or her more conscious of it, more responsible for having it and for getting rid of it. You do this by saying something like: "Honey, there you go again. You're jealous and suspicious. You really *could* do something about that, you know. I've suggested you talk to a counselor. Haven't you done that yet? Or if you don't want to do that, how about reading a book that could help you understand your feelings? Or would you prefer to listen to a cassette tape on the subject of jealousy? My friend mentioned one to me and I'm sure I can find out where we could buy it."

Don't laugh. I know as well as you do that before you can get even half of those statements expressed you're likely to get a barrage of angry and indignant insults thrown right back at you. No matter. You are in the right. Back off if you feel that is the safe course to follow for the moment. However, do not change your strategy. When the occasion arises again that you are being given the third degree, focus on the jealousy again.

On those subsequent occasions don't hesitate to expand your advice with such remarks as:

1. "Dear, why do you still insist on saying I make you jealous? You know no one can upset you unless you allow it. People can only hurt each other physically, not emotionally."

2. "Dear, please stop accusing me of making you jealous by my not always paying complete attention to you. It is the way you talk to yourself *about* my paying attention to others that bothers you. It is never my talking to others. If the act of my paying attention to others could literally cause you to be jealous, then it would have to make me jealous too, wouldn't it, when you pay attention to others? Do you see me get all upset if you talk to others? Of course you don't. Therefore, how can you say that my talking to others upsets you, but when you do the same it doesn't affect me?"

To make that point even more powerful, suggest an analogy such as the following: "If we both get rained on at a picnic, we both get wet, because rain is physical and can soak us both whether we choose to get wet or not. However, whether we get *upset over the soaking* depends entirely on how we think about it. If you tell yourself that getting wet is tragic, unfair, or is going to give you pneumonia, then you'll probably get upset. If I decide that getting soaked is *only* frustrating, *only* an annoyance, *only* regrettable, I won't like it but I won't be seriously upset. It's all in how we interpret the soaking, or, in your case, not getting all the attention you want."

Do not expect this rational talk to have much effect on your partner at first, and perhaps never, for that matter. Still, unless you try, you'll never know whether your constant teaching will eventually sink in.

3. "Dear, if you want to stop those jealous feelings as badly as you insist you do, why don't *you* do something about them? Leave me out of your problem. You insist I should do this or that to give you peace of mind. Yet you do pitifully little for yourself about your own problems. Your jealousy and possessiveness is *your* problem, not mine. What, for example, would you do if instead of being pained by jealousy, you were pained by a toothache? Surely you wouldn't expect me to go to the dentist, or to take a pain-killer, would you? *Nothing I could do* to myself would fundamentally help your toothache, would it? It's precisely the same with your jealousy problem. If I stay home, or show you endless attention, or never talk to another soul in the world, or give you endless sympathy because of your suffering, absolutely nothing that is causing your jealousy will change in you. You'll feel better for a short while, but your insecurity will only rise later to threaten you again because *you*

haven't done anything about *your* sense of inferiority or your childish demand that you have to have everything you want."

These are long-winded responses that you're seldom, if ever, going to get the chance to express as straightforwardly as I've just described. However, you can get a good idea from these three paragraphs of what you *can* say from time to time even if you can only get those ideas out a fragment at a time. Your jealous partner will not like these comments, because it places responsibility for change where it belongs. And, because jealousy problems are often deep and profound, any gains you make will be slow in coming. So be patient. But do not be sidetracked from this strategy. If you are, the problem will almost surely get worse.

The next interview is with a man who associated professionally with three men his wife disapproved of because of their sexually loose ways, and with a female fellow employee.

CLIENT: We were at a party once and Joe said something to me that my wife didn't hear clearly. She asked me later if he made a remark about one of the office girls, but I didn't remember right off which remark she was referring to. After Emma pestered me about it five or six times, I did remember.

Well, that started her off again. "If you can remember now, why couldn't you remember then?" she kept asking.

She does that often. She can remember every word of every conversation she's ever had, I swear it. If my answers deviate the slightest when they're repeated four, five, or six times, she'll latch on to that minor

108

change and we're off again.

THERAPIST: You can never satisfy her questions. That's why I don't want you to keep answering them. Because the only thing she will believe is an admission of guilt. A "yes" answer is the only one she will believe. If she asks: "Are you looking at other women? Do you hate me? Do you have thoughts about other women? Do you want to marry somebody else? Have you been unfaithful?" the only answer she will accept is a "yes" answer.

C: I have given her an option. I have said, "If that's what it takes to make you happy, I will confess anything as long as you get mad, forgive me, and get it all over and done with." I say I will confess to anything she wants if that will solve it. But she won't accept that either.

T: She wouldn't believe that either.

C: Another problem is I have a female working with me. My wife can't believe that I'm not interested in her. I am not trying to say everything I do is right and my wife is always wrong. I don't even want to insinuate that. But I am from the old school. I'm not a flirt, I don't pinch women, and I don't think that women who allow this sort of thing get ahead in their work.

T: O.K., but then you see here again that the only answer she will accept is a guilty answer.

C: It's the only one that seems to satisfy her.

T: I would say, "Look, if the only answer you are going to accept is a guilty one, then why do you ask?"

C: I will even tell her something that I know is going to make her mad, because I don't want to get caught in a lie. For example, she insisted that I not go out to lunch with Joe and Abe. I have done it on occasion and I have told her about it and I always know there is going to be a blowup. I go through hell for about twenty-four to forty-eight hours, but I always tell her.

T: If I were you, I would continue doing as you are. I would not let her nervousness or her jealousy dictate to you. You start doing that and you're going to build a wall around yourself. Don't let her run your life and ruin it. Remember, this is her problem and she has to take care of it and if she won't, she'll have to accept the consequences. I would talk to women. I would conduct my life normally and ethically. If she wants to know what's going on, I would tell her. How she responds is her problem, not yours. Do not upset yourself just because *she doesn't trust herself.* She says she can't trust you. That's malarkey. She can't trust herself. Throw the responsibility right back into her lap and say: "Honey, you have a problem. You want me to do a great deal about your problem. I can't. You have the jealousy, I don't. I can't create jealousy for you. So, since you are creating all of this jealousy and uncertainty for yourself, why don't you do something about it?"

If Talk Fails, Act

Often the most reasonable arguments fall on deaf ears. Sooner or later you will want to increase the pressure on your partner to do something about the jealousy problem. I already suggested one thing you might use to indicate that you are not going to make the requested changes: remain silent and do not answer third-degree questions beyond a few civil and polite responses.

Other actions that you can take are: leave the room,

110

take a walk, go for a drive, or even leave the house overnight or over the weekend if you can. This is especially recommended if you think you are in physical danger. That's why I often suggest that women save some money or keep a credit card handy, so that they can go to a motel at a moment's notice, get a quiet room, and let tempers cool off.

At first this may intensify the friction. I can't help that. Things often get worse before they get better. When you choose Option No. 2, you are declaring a strike and that's usually unpleasant while it lasts. So strong is this act, however, that your mate is likely to realize that you will not allow yourself to be victimized any longer, and if a pleasant relationship with you is desired again, a change will have to be made or *your* behavior will get even worse.

All sorts of accusations will be thrown at you when you behave in what will surely be regarded as unfair, cruel, and uncaring ways. You'll be accused of being selfish, always getting your way, callously destroying the marriage, upsetting the children, being a crazy women's libber or a male chauvinist.

It makes no difference what you are called. Ask yourself honestly if the accusations are true or false. If true, apologize and give in. If false, ignore them and do what your judgment tells you to do.

The accusation that you're behaving crazily needs additional comment. When you hear this said of you, take it as a sign of progress. If you know deep in your heart that you're right, be glad if your partner thinks you're nuts. After all, how can a person reason with someone who is insane? Your mate won't think you've literally lost your mind, only that you've become so unreasonable that further fighting is pointless because your mind is closed. When that happens, it could mean you've won. And if your expectations are not unreasonable, both of you win. What could be better?

Actions speak louder than words, and strong actions speak loudest of all. Therefore, if mild acts of protest don't get your partner to change, try stronger ones.

If you are threatened physically, do what you can to pour oil on the stormy scene. If you are struck, don't necessarily fight back. Wait until your partner is away from you and you can safely call the police. Press charges for arrest. That's right! If you don't, if you allow such behavior to go by unpenalized, you're going to be threatened again. Never mind what the neighbors say. Your life and health are more important than their opinions.

What if your mate comes back from the police station and attacks you? Get into a safe situation and press charges for assault and battery once again. It'll make or break your relationship. It's a chance you may want to take, because the alternative of doing nothing is even worse.

What if the police insist they don't want to get mixed up in a family quarrel? Too bad that this often happens. At least you have shown how far you will go, and that can be very sobering.

If need be, you can always resort to the final choice open to you: separation or divorce. I usually advise separation first to show your spouse how serious you think things are. A separation, to be effective, however, ought to be of several months' duration. When you leave for a week and then return without proof that a fundamen-

112

tal change in your partner has been made, the situation will often deteriorate back to where it was.

Now *You* Consider Your Four Options

Just as your jealous lover always has four options to choose from in dealing with you, so you too have the same four options. For example, if your partner asks you not to stay out too late after your golf game, and even if you think this request is motivated out of jealousy, by all means give in if it will bring a quick peace and if you don't mind the little sacrifice. That's resorting to Option No. 1 (Toleration Without Resentment).

Every request a jealous person makes of us is not automatically unreasonable. Though jealous persons may become neurotic when it comes to losing total attention from their loved ones, they can nevertheless be sensible and stable in a hundred other situations. I've known powerful executives of large corporations who were models of stability, charm, sophistication, and humor, and who ran their lives with consideration for others but who definitely lost their cool if their wives or girl friends shared their attention with other men. We all have an Achilles' heel which always serves as a reminder of just how human we are. Therefore, let's not be hard-nosed about every unreasonable request made upon us. There are a great many times when giving in helps the relationship enormously. Sometimes it is so comforting to the jealous lover that no further protest is registered even when that act is repeated later.

May was gorgeous and outgoing. Before marrying Joe she had a few romances which eventually turned into just friendships. She wanted to continue these after being married to Joe, but he couldn't accept that. She made all the logical arguments to him and to me why she had a right to have male as well as female friends. She also reminded him time after time that he knew before marrying her that she had these associations, enjoyed them, and was by nature a sociable and friendly person. So what right did he have now, after their marriage, to interfere?

I agreed with her completely. Still I reminded her to think over carefully whether she could tolerate his request, wrong as it was, without resentment. She decided to do just that, fortunately. He felt relieved, more sure of her, and eventually relaxed his request and never again felt threatened by her lunching with an ex-boyfriend. Option No. 1 saved the day!

It's only when what is demanded is grossly unfair that you want to protest verbally or with decisive actions. Even if you go below your JRC level from time to time, I still don't recommend that you go on strike. However, if you feel *chronically* cheated, then, and not until then, do I recommend that you assert yourself in this powerful way. Don't start a war over a trivial issue. The consequences and the upheaval of going to Option No. 2 (Strike) are too serious to be taken lightly. Wait until you feel you are being treated so badly that you have the right to create havoc. Then Option No. 2, and nothing short of it, can do the job.

The same advice can be given about resorting to separation or divorce. Separation in particular may well bring back some sense to your demanding lover. Or it can introduce a pain which arises from disappointment and distrust, leaving a wound so deep it cannot easily be healed for a long time.

114

To avoid Option No. 4 (Toleration With Resentment), it is imperative that you use a great deal of common sense and knowledge of psychology. Most people are lacking in both. To correct the first shortcoming, you would have to relive your childhood with different parents, different brothers, sisters, and friends—and that's impossible. To correct the second shortcoming, read books on self-help psychology. For the present I want to focus on those particular emotional hang-ups which you will need to understand if you are to deal successfully with your jealous and possessive partner.

Never Pity the Person You Wish to Change

When you want to change your romance, but gentle discussions don't do the job, you will have to act time after time in forceful ways. This can be difficult for you. When you confront a severely jealous person, you are dealing with one of the world's most rigid personalities. Weaken once and you lose ground that you'll only have to win again. The psychological problem you do not need at that time is called *other-pity*.

In plain language that means feeling sorry for the other person. Don't confuse that with compassion. It's one thing to care about the pain another person goes through as someone tries to modify the person's behavior, but it's an entirely different thing to pity that person. When you pity someone, you care so much for the person's discomfort that you forget your own. This is no time to be neurotically generous.

Recently I was talking to a young man who was shaking and sobbing because his jealous father put his passive mother in the hospital for the third time. For years her children had been telling her to have him arrested, or to leave him, or to do something besides put up with his abuse. Every time she had divorce papers drawn up he would plead with her to change her mind. He used every standard strategy in the book:

> "It was your fault."
> "I promise I'll never hurt you again."
> "You owe me another chance after all I've done for you."
> "I'll kill myself."
> "Think of the children."

That artillery barrage of self-pitying and guilt-provoking statements she could never manage. That weakness ruined the best years of her life.

These victims lack self-assertion skills. What they call generosity and love is in actuality cowardice. It comes from five fears—two are physical, three are psychological in nature: (1) physical punishment, (2) financial loss, (3) being mistaken, (4) hurting the other person's feelings, and (5) rejection.

1. *Physical harm.* Up to a point it makes perfectly good sense to be concerned about being beaten. The battered wife is not an object of humor, she is the subject of great concern. To give in, therefore, to a lover who attacks when frustrated makes good sense.

However, when submitting to violence gets you nowhere and makes your life miserable and no improvement is in sight, why give in? You get beat up if you don't make waves, and you get beat up if you do. So why not take your chances and assert yourself? What have you to lose? When your health is in danger, go down fighting or get out of the arrangement.

Some methods of coping that have worked (according to my clients) are: striking back, calling the police, or seeing a divorce lawyer. Many men tell their wives, "If you don't like it here, don't let the door hit you on the backside as you leave!"

Yet, these same tough men sometimes crumble into crying, frightened boys when they realize that their wives mean business and really are going to leave. When you realize how scared the jealous person is, you will not be surprised if he does a complete about-face the moment you stand up for yourself. Women are often amazed at how quickly their inconsiderate husbands start bringing them flowers when they know the jig is up. These men need their wives a lot more than the women need them. Ladies, you have more power than you ever dreamed of. Use it, and you may be amazed at how quickly the tables are turned. Many women I have counseled have later told me: "I could have put a stop to his tyranny years ago and I didn't do it. I could kick myself."

This is obviously a delicate maneuver. Most women gain greater respect and freedom by rebelling against violence. It must be confessed, however, that in some cases the rebellion may bring on even worse beatings. It's a chance usually worth taking, but be aware of the odds at all times.

2. *Financial loss.* Again this is mainly a fear that women have of men, because men often manage the purse strings. Wisely, many women put up with an unhappy marriage because they fear being put out on the streets penniless. Men often threaten them with precisely these moves, in addition to threatening to take custody of the children.

Much of this is bluff. It is not up to the man to decide

117

whether he will get the children or will leave his wife destitute. Again, women have more rights than they believe, especially with society's changing attitudes toward women.

I suggest that you ladies are lying who keep telling yourselves and others that you are staying married because you "still love him." You are more interested in economic security than in romance. See a lawyer and find out from *him or her,* not your mate, what the chances will be for getting child support and child custody. The effort will often be revealing and rewarding.

3. *Fear of being wrong.* So you're not sure you have a right to bring pressure for this or that. So what! If you wait until you are sure before you act, you'll never act. Ask yourself instead if your frustration is making you *(a)* neurotically disturbed, *(b)* fall out of love, or *(c)* hate the relationship to the point where you want to leave. Is your answer positive to even one of those three questions? If so, you had better talk yourself out of thinking that your mate's desires and needs are all that important. It is time for you to fight for more satisfaction no matter how your partner feels.

If your partner wants to divorce you rather than make you reasonably content, accept the divorce. If you don't do it then, the day will come anyway when you'll get so fed up that you'll get the divorce.

Another point: What's so wrong with making a mistake? Isn't that how we all learn? Your wife doesn't hesitate to push for her way, even though it isn't possible to prove who is right. So why can't you take the same risk? If you find that you're unreasonable to expect her to stay home all the time, change your mind, apologize, and let her have more freedom.

118

If you've been unreasonable by never allowing your husband time to himself, do the same. Only by attempting a course of action can you be somewhat sure you're right or wrong. So take a chance. You're human. You can't be perfect. The proof of the pudding is in the eating. Have a go at it and let's see what happens.

4. *Fear of hurting someone's feelings.* As I have shown before, you cannot hurt people emotionally, only physically. You have never hurt, and can never hurt, adults emotionally. If your mate cries, pouts, gets depressed or angry, never accept responsibility for those emotions. You provide the frustrations. That's true. You did not tell her you loved her. You did not show him enough attention, and so on. Those are frustrations. Whether they will be converted into *disturbances* depends almost entirely on how the frustrations are perceived. The partner who says, "Poor me," will get depressed. The partner who says, "I can't stand not getting my way," will become angry. The partner who says, "This is horrible, I can't stand it," will become nervous and worried.

Notice, these are all self-talk statements. You are only indirectly responsible for them in that you provide the frustration. You are not to blame if that frustration becomes an emotional problem. It surely doesn't have to if the person chooses not to take the event in an upsetting manner.

Stand your ground when you feel you are right. To make that easier, say to yourself: *"That's your problem. If you don't like your emotional pain, don't say irrational things to yourself. Don't blame me for what you are doing to yourself."*

119

5. *Fear of being rejected.* This is probably the greatest fear of all (see *Overcoming Worry and Fear*). It is incredible how frightened some persons are over an experience which, in most cases, is truly nothing more than inconvenient, sad, and regrettable. Yet, mature men and women the world over act as though they were small children when it seems they might not be loved. They become depressed, angry, jealous, or scared to death. Why? Because someone dear to them doesn't love them for a short while or perhaps forever. That is not painful unless you make it hurt. Your self-talk is what makes it such a distressful experience. Carefully think over your irrational thoughts about having to be loved. Accepting yourself with your strengths and weaknesses is the healthiest thing you can do for yourself. Having others like you is perfectly fine, but it doesn't compare with your own *self-acceptance.* I'm not referring to self-love, which involves a judgment of yourself, approving what you do that is good. That's not good enough. To be healthy, you had better learn to accept yourself *whether you do well or badly.* Then and only then will you truly form a stable self-concept.

In other words, you feel upset at the thought of not being loved, because you think that proves you're unworthy. You reason that if you did amount to something, you'd be loved. We rational emotive therapists believe you would not get upset over rejection if you did not reject yourself. That's really the problem. You aren't even a friend to yourself, although you expect others to befriend you at all times. That's what jealous persons do. They reject themselves because others don't love them. All they have to do is not love themselves, *only accept themselves.* That's the partial key to

120

inner strength. And that doesn't mean to resign yourself to your faults. It means to accept your faults if you can't change them now or forever. If you're shorter than you like, reject your size but don't reject yourself. That's self-acceptance. Maybe others will reject you for your size. You'll normally feel sad if that happens, but not inferior. If you think you're no good because you're small, fat, ugly, untalented, black, white, yellow, female, etc., then you'll get hurt when someone rejects you because of those features.

Rejection is also not all that serious when you recall how often you've already broken up with sweethearts and eventually always recovered.

Lastly, how can you seriously believe that your lover is truly indispensable to you when obviously you would not die if you lost the person? All you need in life you probably already have: food, shelter, and clothing. It's wonderful to be in love, but it is *not* a life-and-death matter. You will die without food, shelter, and clothing. You can live without love.

When you look over this matter of rejection carefully, you'll overcome your fear of it and become an assertive human being in the bargain.

Don't Excuse Behavior Because It Started in Childhood

All that I have suggested so far about protesting unacceptable behavior requires a solid conviction on your part that such action may do some good. It is this conviction which gives you the right to put pressure on your mate in the first place. One of the most powerful counterforces that could prevent you from exerting all the pressure is the belief that your mate's behavior comes from childhood days and therefore can't be modified or helped.

If you let that reasoning persuade you, your chances of sticking to your program are very slim. Before you know it, you will be feeling sorry when you would be better off getting tough. You'll recall that your husband was a lonely child and that's why he is so upset when you don't show him enough attention. Or that your wife had an alcoholic father who loved her sister more than her and that's why your wife gets so upset when you dance with other women.

These analyses may well be true. However, don't let them alter your course. They are irrelevant. They don't matter. They only explain why that problem exists, not what you can do about it. Therefore, let it not stop you for a moment as you pressure your lover to change.

In fact, rather than argue that someone who had a disturbed childhood should be treated with *fewer* frustrations, you would be much wiser to argue *for more frustrations* for those persons. How in heaven's name are troubled people to change if we don't make them uncomfortable as they are? People change most often, not because they want to change, but because someone is applying pressure and forcing them to move. What better reason could you have for ignoring their backgrounds? Those who are the most disturbed require the most correction. By ignoring this, we allow them to remain inferior, infantile, spoiled, defensive, and jealous. How kind is that?

To be of real help to your disturbed partner, don't make endless excuses for the person's actions. Don't pity and sympathize. It will only make matters worse.

122

Other-pity almost always encourages self-pity.

Take a hard-nosed attitude about temper tantrums, crying, defensiveness, demanding attention. Be intolerant of those behaviors just as you would be of body odor. To argue that the person "can't help it" or "has always been that way" doesn't do a thing to combat the smell. A shower does, whether it's voluntary or forced.

People can change. The fact that a person has had a problem for the past thirty years does not mean that that problem has to continue. It only means that a powerful habit has been built up over the years. What was learned can be unlearned. That includes smoking, drinking, biting fingernails, correcting a tennis serve, or removing jealous feelings.

Those feelings are part of your psychological system because you talked to yourself for years like a person who made too much of being loved and so you felt worthless unless you were loved. And every time you say that nonsense today, you'll feel jealous and inferior again.

Your partner's jealousy isn't due to having been an adopted child or a middle child, or anything like that. The jealousy comes from what your partner is saying *today* about those past conditions. And if that nonsense is not repeated today, neither is the jealous feeling. By changing how you talk to yourself every day, you can learn to change your reactions either quickly or gradually. But you *can* change and *so can your partner.* Don't forget that if you want to help your neurotic partner.

Seldom Give Unconditional Love

Do you believe that when you love someone you ought to love unconditionally? That's what you may

123

have felt when you took your wedding vows. The implication is clear that there are no ifs, ands, or maybes about falling in love. You either love completely or you don't love at all. To suggest that love has conditions is thought of as irreligious by those who believe marriages are made in heaven and the stork brings babies.

As I see it, love is usually conditional. If your deepest desires and needs are being met to a reasonable degree by someone, you will have a great urge to fall in love. Not to do so requires the strongest self-control.

So what's new about that? Nothing really. That's why people say "love is blind." The opposite will also not come as a surprise either: fail to satisfy your partner's deepest desires and needs, and love diminishes.

There you have it—the fact that love is conditional. Most people believed it all along but never admitted it to themselves. In effect, this view means that "if you satisfy me, I'll love you; if you don't, I won't." This means love is very self-centered and depends almost totally on what you're getting from your lover.

For example, the reason you find yourself falling out of love with your jealous mate is that you do not enjoy being constantly harassed for doing nothing that you regard as out of line. Being harassed is not among your deepest desires or needs. And when your partner doesn't satisfy those conditions, love flies out of the window.

Therefore, do not feel guilty for falling out of love. It happens for two reasons, both reasonable: *(a)* your deepest desires and needs have changed but your partner cannot meet these new expectations, or *(b)* they have not changed but were not reasonably satisfied for a long time.

To prevent this development, decide to forget your

frustrations or protest hard enough so that such frustrating behavior ceases. In that way, by putting conditions on your love, you shape your lover's behavior in a direction that pleases you and makes your partner more like the person you can love.

Therefore, do not apologize for wanting your lover to change. Why shouldn't you want change? If you get no real satisfaction from the relationship, then change had better be made. When the charge is made to you: "Why can't you love me the way I am? If you loved me, you wouldn't want me to change," pay no attention. You won't love your partner unless there are changes, because you understand love as a business transaction with conditions to the contract. As for the second charge: "If you loved me . . .," that won't hold water either. You can always counter that protest with another one, "If *you* really loved me, you wouldn't object to my wanting a few changes from you."

Are You Incompatible?

You are not likely to go through the tough program I've written about unless you feel your marriage is worth it. It is worth it if you believe you are compatible. Why else would you want to tolerate a relationship unless you thought it could lead to happiness for both parties?

How can you tell if you and your lover are compatible? Ask yourself three questions. If you get one "no" answer, consider yourself incompatible.

First question: Does your lover *understand* what your deepest desires and needs are?

Second question: Is your lover *able* to satisfy your

deepest desires and needs?

Third question: Is your lover *willing* to satisfy your deepest desires and needs?

Even a brief study of these questions will quickly show why a negative answer means incompatibility. How can your partner make you happy if he or she doesn't *know* what you require, is *unable* to please you, or would *refuse* even if able to please you? Obviously, no happy marriage is possible unless these three conditions are met. If they are not met, do something about it and perhaps you can become compatible.

Fight Jealousy with Jealousy

Remember the case in Chapter 2 of the woman who was so jealous she drove away about ten male friends? She had a unique experience. She was treated jealously by the lover whom *she* was always jealous of. That single act was powerful enough to wake her up and expose her to her irrational fears. She saw her jealousy pattern clearly for the first time.

CLIENT: One night I talked to a fellow that I went to college with, and Benny didn't say anything about it. But then, after he heard that I got candy at work, he just went into a rage and imagined that I had done all sorts of things. When I came home from work he would immediately jump on me in a mean sort of way. He would say, "Well, did you see your boyfriend today?" That's how he refers to this guy. Doesn't ask his name or anything but just calls him that, and it was just driving me nuts. I did not want to go home. I thought for a while I was going to have to move out.

126

I tried to be understanding of him. I tried to say: "Look, nothing happened. It may look a lot worse than it is, but nothing happened. It's done with. You might as well forget it."

And then it got so I lost my patience and wasn't understanding anymore. If he started that, I just walked out of the room and ignored him. It wasn't doing any good to be understanding. But last night he did sort of drop it. I don't know why, but he kind of forgot it.

THERAPIST: What did you think this whole thing taught you?

C: How you can drive persons away by accusing them of things they're not doing. Even if there's nothing going on, you can make that person want to leave you.

T: Tell me what you felt.

C: I felt I didn't want to go home. At first it made me mad that he would gripe at me like that. Well, first I felt guilty, because in a way I suppose I did encourage this college friend. After that, I just got sick of hearing about it. It was over, I did not want to hear it anymore. And when it came time to go home from work and I knew I was going to have to listen to that, it actually made me physically ill. If he hadn't quit it when he did, I think I would have had to move out.

T: You really got a good taste of what it's like to live with a jealous person. This time it's he who is jealous, not you.

C: Yeah.

T: Does that really open your eyes a little bit?

C: Yes, it sure does.

T: Do you think that can change your behavior?

127

C: I can really see how you can drive a person away when nothing has happened.

A Client Who Opted for Divorce

THERAPIST: Tell me what it is like living with a jealous person, what he does and how you feel, and that sort of thing.

CLIENT: I think he feels inadequate. He can't keep me home. If I went to church with the kids, he would really get upset because I wouldn't stay home with him. He wants my total attention. I kept telling myself that he would grow out of it, because we were married so young, but he never did. Things just got worse, never better. They just get worse.

T: You have been married about fifteen years?

C: Yes.

T: And things haven't improved?

C: No, they have just gotten worse. I can't talk on the phone. I talk to my brother and my husband says: "What were you talking about? Were you talking about me?" And I say, "No." I would end up losing no matter what I said.

T: How do you mean you would lose?

C: He would get very angry and that scared me. I was afraid that he would hit me. If I talked to my brother or anybody, he would say I was talking about him even if I wasn't. He would get upset with me. So I was afraid to talk to anybody. Even if I said what he wanted me to say, "O.K., you're right, that's what I was doing," he would say, "I knew you were." We would go round and round. There was no way to win.

T: In other words, if you agreed to his accusations, he

128

got mad and beat you up; and if you denied his accusations, he got mad because he was convinced you were lying and he beat you up. You couldn't win.

C: Right. So I want a divorce. I can think of no way I can win.

T: Perhaps you ought to make the move as soon as possible. If you don't, first of all, you will only continue your anxiety, worry, and fear of being hurt. That's going to accomplish nothing good for you. Secondly, if you delay, you give him false hopes. He may think you are changing your mind. Do you notice that?

C: Yes. He thinks I am going to stay there, but I think I have to get the divorce. I get real anxious about that and then he comes and says: "Why don't you drop that divorce? You aren't going to get it." He doesn't believe me, and I don't blame him for not believing me, because I have never acted. I have always just said, "I will, I will," but I never did. Now I want to.

T: Why are you suddenly doing it now? Why are you more determined now?

C: I want more from the marriage.

T: But you wanted it before. Why are you taking the final step now in moving toward divorce? You wanted this before, but you really never stood up for yourself. Why now?

C: Because I have learned more.

T: How did you learn more?

C: By reading your books. You helped me see how incompatible we are. I kept telling myself that he would change, that he would grow out of this. Finally I stopped saying that. He doesn't have to change. There is nothing to say that he has to change. He can stay like this forever. I thought I had better do something if I don't want that.

T: Did you begin to say, "If he is going to be this way forever, I'd better do something about getting out of here?"

C: Yes. I was waiting for him to change. I kept saying he would change eventually, he would grow out of this.

T: May I suggest that if things are that bad and you really feel you no longer love your husband, you get a divorce as soon as you possibly can? He's dangerous.

C: That is what I want to do, because of the anxiety the marriage is creating. But I am fearful that more anxiety is going to be created once I file for divorce.

T: That's right. You will become more anxious.

C: But I know that is not a catastrophe.

T: That's right, it is not a catastrophe. You will be more nervous until this thing is finally over. But it is easier to face it than to run away from it. Let's go through with it although it is going to be a very tense time. If you don't get the divorce, what is going to happen, finally?

C: Apparently he is not going to stop his behavior. He has already said that in his actions, not in his words. He will say almost anything after he feels regretful. He will say something like, "I'm sorry, I'll never irritate you again as long as I live." You know the routine that you go through every time.

T: So you don't want that to be your future? Take the risk now and end this thing. It's the chance you take, because I don't know how disturbed this man is. It may be a good thing for him to lose his marriage. It may cause him to say, "I do have a problem, and I

130

ought to do something about it."

Until someone stands up to him and stops giving in to him, and letting him get by with this behavior, he will go on and on. There is no reason for him to change. So I say, go to a lawyer, get out of this marriage, and save your neck.

C: You mean go ahead and feel anxious. I know it is not going to hurt me to feel anxious for a while.

T: You will probably be anxious and upset as long as the divorce is in process. But after it is over with and he realizes you mean business, and you have some control over the situation, he may eventually let you alone. Then the anxiety will drop off, because now you are in control again and you have done something about the problem.

C: To be in control of my life again would be nice.

T: That's right.

I saw this client six weeks later. Her remarks are so typical of what happens to persons seeking a separation or divorce that I want to share part of that session with you.

T: You have now gotten your divorce? Correct?

C: Yes.

T: What is he doing now?

C: Now he wants me back again, and wants me to date him. He wants to stay with me. I told him: "Look, we're divorced. Think of me as dead, and I will do the same." It was tough for me to say "no." In my heart, "yes," but my head is saying: "No way. Knock it off." But emotionally I would just like to grab him and hug him and say, "Yes, anything you want." That's a battle between me and myself.

131

T: What are you telling yourself when you say, "Oh, gee, wouldn't it be nice if I could love the man again"?

C: I've asked myself that before. I think of all his good points. He's a generous person, he's warm, he's affectionate and caring. I tell myself all these nice things about him. On the other hand, I ask, "How much of that is me?" I'm scared of this guy who has beat me up many times, once severely. "Are you really giving this guy the shaft? Are you really giving him a hard time?" I ask myself all sorts of little questions like that. And I always come up with: "Yes, he's a very attractive man, he's everything I would want in a husband, but he hits me. And he gets angry, and I'm afraid of anger."

T: Do you think he can change that?

C: I don't know.

T: Can I give you some pointers? He might outgrow this when he reaches middle age. If you want to wait that long, you may have a few broken noses in the process. There is no guarantee. Secondly, if he doesn't outgrow it by himself, he ought to get into counseling. But even then a jealous person has to work on the problem. If he doesn't, you won't have a different man than you had before. He's coming on nice and sweet now, with candy and flowers. He's a real lover and he's very attentive. But he's the same guy. He is still as jealous and insecure as he ever was. And if you didn't like that jealousy before, you're not going to like it tomorrow if you change your mind about the divorce. My point to you is to let it be.

C: That's very hard.

T: I'll tell you what's harder. Say "yes" to him.

132

C: Yes, well, I didn't think so last night. It would have been easier to say "yes" last night.

T: It seems like it would have been easier just for the moment.

C: It would have been terrific for the evening. But the next day he would have knocked at my door and followed me from room to room again. I can't deal with that anymore. I can deal with it, but I don't want to deal with it.

T: So what do you plan on doing?

C: I am going to have to be strong and keep saying "no."

T: If he calls you, what are you going to do?

C: I don't know. I think he manipulates me with the kids. If I am not nice to him, he is not going to come and see the kids. I believe that is a cop-out. If he really wanted to see the kids, he would come and see them.

T: Amen. He's using the kids against you?

C: In some way. It is like I can't get him just to see the kids and not involve me.

T: Yes, you can.

C: I can?

T: Just tell him that if he really cares for his kids and he wants to see them, he'll see them whether he sees you or not.

C: He has to come and see me and talk to me. Hold my hand.

T: Why does he say he has to do that?

C: Because it hurts him too much to just turn around and just leave me.

T: Nothing you can do about that now.

C: He said it is never too late.

T: Well, fine, but what is he doing about changing?

133

C: Nothing. His dad is telling me how much I'm hurting him, and everyone is telling me how much I'm hurting him. And he really looks bad. "How can you treat him like that?" That's the way it is, and I can't do anything about that. I just yell at them. I didn't hurt him. He hurt himself.

T: O.K. Now you're making sense.

C: I say it to them, but I don't know if I buy it inside.

T: I don't care if you buy it or not. Keep saying it. Keep saying it to him. Keep saying it to yourself until you finally hear it enough times that you begin to accept it. You cannot upset other people emotionally.

C: That is the hardest thing for me to buy.

T: You're a pitier. You pity people too much. You not only care for them, you *pity* them. You're not good for them that way. That's why this guy comes on very strong, because he knows he can make you feel sorry for him. He knows exactly what to do. You are an other-pitier, not a self-pitier.

C: That's what I'm beginning to think I am. Sometimes I think I feel sorry for myself.

T: That's not your major problem. The big difficulty you have is feeling sorry for others. And especially when he comes along and moans and groans, and you begin to forgive everything. Don't listen to any part of this. Don't feel sorry for him. He wants you to feel sorry for him so that you will come through and change your mind, and let him back into your life.

C: And not to believe that I hurt him, he's hurting himself. I don't hurt other people's feelings. I think I still believe that people can hurt my feelings. I know it is not true, but it is hard to swallow inside.

T: It is hard to be convinced of that because you're not

134

thinking about it. Other people can hurt you physically but cannot hurt you emotionally.

C: I'd say that my getting a divorce was a frustration.

T: To your husband mainly.

C: But I'm not hurting him?

T: You're not disturbing him.

C: I'm not disturbing him, O.K., but I'm hurting him in the sense that he's not getting his goals in life, right?

T: Right, and *then* he makes himself miserable because he is not reaching his goals in life. Does he have to make himself miserable and all upset and angry because he is not getting what he wants? Do *you* always get angry, miserable, depressed when you don't get what you want? When you get frustrated you don't change every frustration into a disturbance, do you?

C: Not usually, not this time.

T: Now, who's problem is that?

C: I'm not sure.

T: That's *his* problem.

C: It's hard for me to differentiate between what's my problem and his problem.

T: No, the thing to differentiate between is what is the frustration and what is the disturbance. The frustration is . . .

C: The frustration is that I've removed him legally from my home.

T: That's the frustration to your husband.

C: And then he gets hurt because his goals are not being achieved. Then he chooses to get disturbed over it.

T: Lots of people get all sorts of frustrations, and they

135

don't get disturbed over them. If they don't get disturbed over the frustration, then obviously it can't be a frustration that is disturbing people. It must be the way that they are *looking* at the frustration, the way they interpret it, the way they *react* to it. He reacts typically to frustrations in a very immature, angry, depressed, self-pitying way. That's why he get's so upset. And he says, "Poor me."

C: He wants me to give to him what he won't give to himself.

T: Which is?

C: Love, or something. He won't give himself any acceptance.

T: That's right, he won't even accept himself. But you're supposed to love him unconditionally when he won't do that for himself. That's why he's so scared every time you talk to somebody. Because he thinks . . .

C: Because he doesn't think he is capable of keeping me. I can't figure out why. Why is he afraid? I didn't do anything. I didn't do anything to make him think that I was going to go out on him. I didn't do anything.

T: What's that got to do with it?

C: I had to do something to bring out his jealousy, didn't I?

T: But you did do something, you received a telephone call from a man. In his book (because he's so threatened) that's enough. That's like the end of the world for him. He probably thought: You've got to love that guy more than me. Who am I anyway? I'm nothing. I don't see how you could love me.

136

C: Apparently anything I considered nonharmful he considered harmful.

T: His wife's talking to a man on the telephone is normally not threatening to almost any man who is reasonably secure. Her dancing with a man, kissing a man occasionally at a social engagement, that's no big thing. Most men can take that. But your husband says: "Nobody can love me. I'm no good. Why should she love me?" You never could convince him of that.

C: I tried that a lot. I worked so hard at that marriage that I think I was probably the nuttier one. I think I'm the crazier one. I worked so hard at it.

T: You weren't the nuttier one. You just couldn't understand why all your hard work wasn't paying off. You simply couldn't understand that he could feel so inferior that nothing you could do could prove to him that you really did care. He didn't care for whom?

C: Himself. He still doesn't. A little bit more now, maybe.

T: Fine, I wish him the very best and hope he gets some education in the psychology of self-acceptance someday.

Summary

I HAVE SEVERAL COMMENTS I WANT TO MAKE TO TWO parties: *(a)* the persons whose jealousy is a problem to themselves as well as *(b)* those who live close to them.

Few emotional disturbances are as painful, constant, or self-defeating as jealousy. If you suffer from the green-eyed monster, you know it. Though you may deny it to high heaven and swear on your mother's grave that you're as solid as a mountain, down deep you know that's psychological cosmetics. You've got a problem, perhaps a serious one, and you and all those close to you know it.

My advice is to be honest with yourself, more honest than you have ever been. There is no disgrace in admitting an imperfection. You have the right—no, even the obligation—to accept yourself despite all that your jealous soul drives you to. You are the victim of unfortunate errors during the years your personality and character were being formed. You are the victim today of ignorance of what causes your suspicions and rages. And you are ignorant of how to overcome them.

Fortunately it is no longer necessary to allow ignorance to destroy your peace of mind and drive away

138

those you love. Psychology has made enormous strides in understanding human behavior. Counseling no longer requires daily sessions for years to make an impact. Counseling is now viewed as a learning experience. People are disturbed because they have been taught to be so. You are jealous because you were trained to be jealous. What you have learned you can unlearn. I find that people are quite ready and willing to learn to run their lives without unnecessary mental distress if only someone will tell them how to do it. That's why I have written this book.

Now for a few comments to those of you who live or work with jealous persons. I believe your greatest contribution toward helping them is to understand the jealous condition and then not to tolerate it.

As I hope I have demonstrated, this condition can be avoided if you use your first three options wisely. Guilt and other-pity are the two major obstacles you will want to avoid. To accomplish this, I urge you to overcome *your* emotional imperfections no less than I urge the jealous client to do the same.

Your emotional hang-ups are merely different from those of jealous persons. You have your own, whatever they are. Some of them are not helpful, and that's why you have not coped successfully with your partner even though you have given it your best efforts for months or years.

It is time you stopped thinking that your jealous companion had all the work to do. Often no progress will be made in conquering jealousy unless you stop tolerating it. When you change, your partner is likely to change, not before.

Both of you now have some of the tools you will need

139

to correct this situation. Work hard, don't become discouraged, read this book again from time to time and underline important sentences. Then apply what you have learned, and I hope you live happily ever after, both of you.

→ ~~973-248~~

The Sport   973 - 589 - 4936
Club   973 - 589 - 5078 (Bar)
    Portobiz   Prospet Str.
          973 - 589 - 1133